The Canoe Handbook

Techniques for mastering the sport of canoeing

Slim Ray

STACKPOLE BOOKS

Published by
STACKPOLE BOOKS
5067 Ritter Road
Mechanicsburg, PA 17055
www.stackpolebooks.com

Printed in the United States of America

First Edition

10 9 8

Illustrated by Andrea K. U'Ren
Cover photo courtesy of Bill Burger/Dagger Canoe

To my mother, Evelyn Ray

Library of Congress Cataloging-in-Publication Data

Ray, Slim.
    The canoe handbook : techniques for mastering the sport of
canoeing / Slim Ray.—1st ed.
        p.   cm.
    Includes bibliographical references (p.) and index.
    ISBN 0-8117-3032-8
    1. Canoes and canoeing—Handbooks manuals, etc. I. Title.
GV783.R35   1992
797.1'22—dc20   91-16032
                                                                CIP
ISBN 978-0-8117-3032-7

Contents

Acknowledgments

BOOKS LIKE THIS are necessarily a cooperative effort, incorporating the knowledge and experience of many people. I wish to acknowledge the invaluable assistance of the Nantahala Outdoor Center for its help in the preparation of this book, especially the members of the Instruction Department, who made their materials and experience available to me. Specifically:

Dave Moccia, NOC head canoe instructor, for his pithy comments and help in shooting.

Gordon Grant, NOC head of instruction, for reviewing the manuscript and offering many valuable suggestions.

Bunny Johns and Janet Smith, for comments and modeling tandem canoe.

Ed Daugherty, for reviewing the manuscript and for making suggestions on strokes.

John Barbour and the NOC Outfitter's Store staff for helping run down a hundred bits and pieces.

Bunny Johns and Ken Kastorff for allowing me to use portions of "Concepts of Paddling."

Kent Ford for making available drafts of "the book that never was" as well as for his reviews and comments.

Dante Langston for letting me use his commentary on river etiquette.

Thanks also to Kathy Bolyn, John "J. R." Reynolds, Kim Fadiman, and the rest of the NOC staff.

Special thanks also to William Nealy and Holland Wallace, Kay Henry and Rob Center of Mad River Canoe, Joe Pulliam and Steve Scarborough of Dagger Canoe, all the good folks at Mohawk Canoe, Bart Parrott and the staff of *Canoe* magazine, Harry Roberts and *Canoesport Journal*, Jamie McEwan, the American Canoe Association (especially Commodore Dave Mason, Joyce Malone, and Tom Foster), and Mike Cichanowski and Rob Linden of We-No-Nah Canoe for all their help and support. Special thanks to Charlie Wilson and Sawyer Canoe's Dana Grover for their help in shooting the freestyle and sit'n'switchers.

Thanks also to Nolan Whitesell for permission to use his rolling article, which originally appeared in *Canoe* magazine. Nolan, the proprietor of Canoes by Whitesell in Atlanta, specializes in custom fitting whitewater canoe instruction as well as uniquely designed whitewater canoes.

Foreword

I ADMIRE Slim Ray for writing a new book on canoeing, but I don't envy him. Writing is hard work, and writing a text on canoeing is deceptively difficult, just as canoeing is—at times—a deceptively difficult sport. Watch a skilled canoeist negotiate a big rapid, moving the boat with precision along a chosen line through the waves and spray, stopping at will in a rhythmic application of style. It looks wonderful, and it is, but how is it taught? What underlies the calculated grace of the expert, and how does one get there?

The author of a manual on canoeing technique and style must wrestle with the same challenge all teachers face: What information is necessary to a student, and how can it be shown most simply and directly? Just like the deceptive ease of an expert boater's strokes, a clearly stated or written instruction is a distillation of experience. The best teachers can condense their wide range of experiences into a single sentence or direction that outlines precisely the choice or movement a student needs to make. But it takes a lot of experience to cook down to that one clear drop of information.

Slim Ray has just such a range of experience, as well as the ability to condense and express the underlying principles he has learned. Throughout his fourteen years as raft guide, canoe and kayak instructor, photo-journalist, and author, he has made his living either on rivers or writing about them. He has run rivers in Europe, Asia, and the Americas, as well as most of the classic white water of North America. These travels, and his position of leadership in international river-safety symposiums, give him as broad a perspective on the sport as anyone today. It is to his credit that he maintains this sense of perspective while living in Wesser, North Carolina, where he is surrounded by as rowdy, talented, and opinionated a group of paddlers as exists anywhere—the guides and instructors of the Nantahala Outdoor Center. Amidst all this, Slim continues to listen to ideas from all sources, from rescue workers in Ohio to members of Europe's Alpine Canoe Club. Each new idea he entertains with a blend of serious attention, humorous practicality, and much testing on the water.

This book, then, is a well-crafted detailing of what Slim has learned. I hope readers use it as a base on which to build their own adventures.

—Gordon Grant
Head of River Instruction
Nantahala Outdoor Center

Introduction

YET ANOTHER BOOK about canoeing? It seems hard to write something new and worthwhile, because in some respects canoeing has changed little since prehistoric times. Transport an Indian from before the time of the white man to ours, put him in a modern whitewater canoe, and give him a high-tech synthetic paddle; he'd probably do a passable job of getting down the river. You can't say that about many other sports (cross-country skiing, perhaps). Ours is a sport steeped in lore and legend, bound inextricably with the history of America, both its native peoples and those who came later. Though this history is useful in establishing a link to America's past, it also tends to give each of us a certain amount of mental and emotional baggage about what canoeing *should* be. Canoes, after all, were, and are, the all-American watercraft. They opened much of this country to exploration when there were no roads, when running rapids was easier and safer than trying to bushwhack through a trackless forest.

But some things have changed a lot. Modern canoeing is almost entirely recreational. Yet even this orientation is not completely new: recreational canoeing was very popular around the turn of the century. The difference today is that canoeing, like many other activities of the eighties and nineties, is being undertaken as a sport. And I don't mean just racing. People train seriously to paddle, and take pride in showing off new strokes and techniques, even to the point of being obnoxious about it. And there are those who, like the freestylers, do new and radical things just to be new and radical. As you would expect, there is often a great deal of concern about what's right and what's not. Sometimes it seems that the pure pleasure of canoeing gets lost in the process.

This is far from the utilitarian world of canoeing as it began. Though native American canoes undoubtedly had some design aesthetics, they were for the most part more analogous to the modern family car or commercial truck. They were work boats, built to carry families, goods, and war parties down the liquid interstates of a vast and primitive land. The same can be said for the canoes of the white traders and voyageurs: design followed function within the limits of the available materials—wood and bark. Later designs, including those of Rushton and others, followed the style of those early canoes even when newer materials became available. Canoe design was much influenced by what went on in the heart of canoe country, the Great North Woods. The romance of Hudson's Bay, of the Couriers du Bois, of pack, paddle, and portage, stamped the face of canoeing indelibly. There are still those folks, like Garrett and Alexandra Conover in Maine, who do it the traditional way.

Canoeing has always attracted strong-minded people. That's a polite way of saying that paddlers are opinionated as hell. They are people who can be wonderfully innovative while looking over their shoulders to see whether what they're doing is still really canoeing . . . and be splendidly individualistic while insisting that everyone else do things exactly the same way. All boaters seem reluctant to break with the past. We still talk of a boat's gunnels, or gunwales, a strip of reinforcing material running down the top of the canoe's sides. The word derives directly from the twelfth-century Middle English word *gonnewale*, or gun wall, from a time in the Middle Ages when this rail was used to prop up the first crude guns.

If you think I'm exaggerating about the pull of tradition, look at what happened in racing. We would think that racing, of all facets of the sport, would be straining toward the future, free from the constraints of the past. Not so. Until the early seventies every racing canoe, whether solo or tandem, had to have the bow higher than the center of the boat, even though the boat had a waterproof deck. The reason? To preserve the traditional "canadien" canoe shape! (In Europe, open canoes are still called canadiens.)

Another example: the traditional upcurved bow of a canoe makes sense when the boat is made with a wooden keel. That's the way wood likes to be shaped. With aluminum, fiberglass, or ABS, it really doesn't matter, but a lot of canoes still look like, well, canoes.

The same thing applies to canoe strokes. Reduced to the essentials, there are only four strokes: forward, backward, and draws or prys to move the boat from side to side. Yet whole books have been written about strokes, including some silly and useless ones. At one time, reverse strokes were considered very important. They were—to loaded tandem canoes, which customarily backferried through rapids. Much of the development of what we may loosely call modern canoeing, however, emphasizes aggressive *forward* paddling, on both flat water and white water. Reverse paddling is also difficult in a solo open canoe, which has lately assumed an important role in the sport. But check the latest edition of the ACA Instructor Manual. The reverse strokes are still there (as they are in this book).

Solo canoeing is definitely one of the new trends. Ten years ago there were few purely solo boats, and most instructional clinics catered to tandem boats. If you wanted to go for bigger water, you took up kayaking. Today there is a whole range of solo boats suitable for almost any purpose, and solo whitewater boats now run just about anything that can be kayaked. Even many couples now go with a pair of solo boats instead of with the traditional tandem canoe.

Boats have become more specialized, in both design and materials. One boat used to go everywhere, do everything. Now it's common for people to own half a dozen (or more) boats: a 'glass Galt freestyler, a fast Yost Kevlar sit'n'switcher, an ABS whitewater boat, and maybe a composite layup tandem boat. Not to mention a kayak or two.

The style of paddling has changed also. Not for us the relaxed, ukelele-strumming cruises or the cautious backferrying of yesteryear. Today (apologies to the shade of Bill Mason) it goes toward aggressive playing and eddy hopping on white water and freestyle demos on flat water. Perhaps this is a reflection of our slightly overheated lifestyle.

Instruction programs have grown with the sport and, like boats and paddlers, tend to specialize in one aspect of the sport or another. One thing is for sure, however, and that is that instruction programs are better than ever, with students learning more in a shorter time than at any time in the past.

However, as canoesport grows larger, the different pieces grow ever further apart, and it begins to strain any book, as it does this one, to include all of them. What I have chosen to emphasize in this book is the sport of paddling as it developed (and continues to develop) at the Nantahala Outdoor Center in the seventies, the eighties, and into the nineties. NOC has been variously described as the Oxford *(Esquire)* and the Julliard *(Outside)* of the paddling world. Though much of NOC's instruction program is a direct extension of what has gone before, the sheer size and scope of the program has led to some instructional innovation. To get information through to a student quickly and clearly, the instructors developed some common teaching principles and a teaching progression that works. Instructors like Dave Moccia and Ed Daugherty have put a great deal of time into making this a consistent, easy-to-learn system. And so it appears in this book. Yes, there is a whitewater orientation in this book. But you move the boat the same way on any water: if you understand a river and how to move the boat, you will be at home anywhere.

What you will not see in this book is a lot of space devoted to the ancillary aspects of canoeing. This book is concerned with the technique of canoeing, not with camping, portaging, or the like. One thing you will see, however, is the seamless integration of safety into canoe technique. Learning what to do outside the boat is as essential as learning what to do while in it. An unavoidable corollary of our aggressive modern style is that we swim more when learning. But that, too, can be a beneficial experience.

There are other perfectly valid systems and methods of canoeing, of course, and I have tried to mention them when appropriate. But you will not find a detailed description of, say, freestyle paddling here. I leave that to the freestylers themselves.

I do not write this book as a guru, either from a mystical standpoint or as a river pontiff. I have recorded what I have found: a method that works on a daily basis.

TIP: DO NOT BELIEVE EVERYTHING YOU READ no matter who the authoritative writer is or what the accepted book or magazine. There are people out there who like to make easy things difficult to understand. Then there are people who dedicate their entire lives to trying to make easy things more simple, and in doing so really muck things up. In other words, if it works for you or works better, use it—and throw the rest of the garbage away.

—Dave Moccia

ONE

Water

WATER. Without it there would be no life as we know it on this planet. Few animals can live without it for more than a few days. It is the most yielding of fluids, finding its way into the smallest of spaces. It sparkles in the sun, providing the most sublime pleasure for those who can connect, by paddle and boat, with its mysteries and power. Yet it has a dual nature. Water can cut great canyons, excavate potholes, and scour away rock. Aroused, it can carry huge trees and boulders along in a terrifying torrent, sweeping away whole cities in the path of a flood. This life-sustaining liquid, which comprises some 70 percent of our body tissues and two-thirds of our weight, can kill an air-breathing creature by depriving it of oxygen. Unfortunately, when people and water are put together, drownings are not just a possibility but a likelihood. Several hundred people drown in a typical year in the United States. A great many of these drownings result directly from ignorance of the ways of water.

It follows that if you want to spend time on the water, be it a lake or a river, flat water or white water, you must know its ways. They are not mysterious. Mark Twain, author and riverboat pilot, compared the river to a book, which, he said, spoke to him "as clearly as if

. . . with a voice," telling him a new story every day. So the first station in our journey—before we talk about boat design, paddles, or canoeing itself—is to learn to listen to the voice of the river. Learn it well, for water can give you both pleasure and sorrow. The voice speaks not just through the thunder of white water: all moving water flows alike. It is simply a question of scale. Look at a tiny brook and you will see exactly the same features as on the mighty Colorado. Read Twain's *Life on the Mississippi* and you'll see that riverboat pilots had the same currents, eddies, and strainers that any paddler must deal with today.

The Nature of Water

For the paddler, water has two important characteristics: *fluidity* and *weight*. Its fluidity allows it to flow around obstructions in its path, seeking the lowest level. Its weight gives it power. Water is surprisingly heavy. Our forefathers, who carried water from well to house, probably appreciated this more than we do. Pick up a gallon jug of water, hold it at arm's length, and you will see what I mean. Now throw the jug at something. It hits with quite a bit of force, doesn't it? That gallon weighs 8.33 pounds, and a cubic foot of water weighs 62.4 pounds. A small river might flow 600 cubic feet per second (often abbreviated as cfs), meaning that a slice of water containing 600 cubic feet of water—37,440 pounds of it—flows past a given point in one second. A large river (or a smaller one in flood) might run over 100,000 cfs. That's a lot of weight. But water doesn't move itself; it takes an outside force to make things happen.

For still water, the usual force is wind. For moving water, it is gravity. For really large bodies of water like oceans, part of the gravity comes from the moon, causing tides. Let's focus on gravity for a moment, since it is the prime mover of rivers. Simply put, water constantly seeks a base level, usually the sea. In other words, water flows downhill. The steeper the gradient, the faster it flows, simultaneously increasing the speed of the current and both the force and the carrying capacity of the water. Gradient is usually expressed in feet or meters per mile, as an average figure over a designated section. This can be deceptive, however, since some rivers give up their elevation gradually at a more or less constant rate; others may have long, flat stretches interrupted by abrupt drops. As the gradient steepens, the force of the river increases *exponentially.* That is, when the speed of the current doubles, the force quadruples (in scientific terms, the force of the water increases in proportion to the square of the velocity of the current). The carrying capacity of a river increases dramatically as the *flow* increases, also cubing as the volume doubles. (For example, if we double the amount of water flowing through a given section with the same gradient, the water can carry three times the amount of debris; double it again and it carries nine times as much.) Rivers in flood carry forty-foot trees like matchsticks and roll boulders like marbles along their beds. This power may not be obvious if you are simply riding along on the surface, but it can be overwhelming if you suddenly stop and it is turned against you.

For the paddler, then, the two most important numbers to determine the characteristics of a river are the *gradient* (how much the river drops: an indication of how much the force of gravity will affect the river) and the *flow* (an indicator of the potential power and carrying capacity of the water). For example, the Colorado River in the Grand Canyon averages 30,000 to 40,000 cfs, but drops only 8 to 10 feet per mile. However, individual rapids may drop 15 to 30 feet in a quarter mile or less, with current speeds up to 10 miles per hour. The Chattooga River on the Georgia–South Carolina border, on the other hand, averages a flow of about 650 cfs, but drops 50 to 60 feet per mile (and nearly 300 feet per mile in one quarter-mile section). Both rivers, although different in character, are rated about the same on the International Scale of Difficulty, which runs from I to VI. This rating system is only a starting point, however. There are many other considerations in determining the difficulty and character of a river, which we will consider in due course.

Flowing Water

Let's look at the way water flows. Water flowing in a smooth riverbed is an example of *laminar* flow. Distinct layers of water move at different speeds, sliding over each other as if on bearings. The fastest current is generally at or near the center and surface of the river, and the slowest near the banks and bottom, where the flow is slowed somewhat by friction. Near the banks, this friction pulls at the passing current, causing the water to spiral along the banks in a *helical* pattern, moving outward along the surface until it reaches the main current, then diving along underneath to return to the bank along the bottom.

The wayward main current, however, does not remain in the center of the river, but instead *meanders* from one bank to another. This is determined partly by the geology of the bed, and partly by the rhythmic laws of hydrodynamics. The length of a meander, for example, is about eleven times the width of the river, and this is the approximate spacing of the river's bends. In general, bigger rivers have longer meanders. Similarly, all rivers alternate to some extent between deep pools and shallow stretches. The main current meanders not only horizontally between the banks but vertically as well, diving into the pools and surfacing in the shallows. Like meanders, the spacing of pools and shallows follows a definite harmonic relationship: three to seven times the width of the river. The shallows are where we would expect to find sandbars—or rapids.

Perhaps this rhythm is one of the things that attracts us to rivers in the first place. It's like music. Some rivers, like the Colorado, have a grand, larger-than-life cadence like a Wagnerian opera. A typical eastern creek run, on the other hand, is a complex jazz number with a quicktime tempo and overlapping layers of sound to a complex syncopated beat. What appears at first to be chaos resolves itself, upon closer scrutiny, into the music of the spheres.

Start with a straight-channeled river: the meandering current, following its own universal laws and defying man and the Army Corps of Engineers, will begin to elbow its banks. What begins as a gentle nudge eventually will wear a bend in the channel. As the water flows around this bend, several important things happen. First, as the curve of the bend increases, the weight and momentum of the water will push it ever more strongly. Water, like any other heavy substance, does not like to change direction, and the steeper the bend, the more abruptly it must turn. This causes the

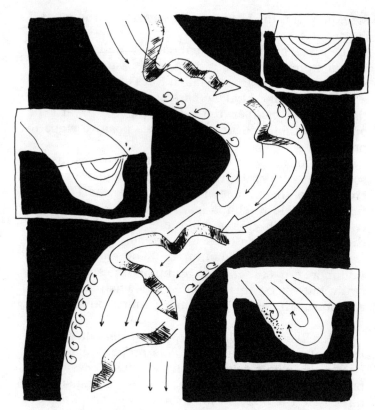

water to pile up on the outside; that is, the water on the outside of the bend flows physically higher than the water on the inside.

Second, this same momentum now slides the fastest current, which started in the middle of the river, against the outside of the bend. The water on the outside of the bend must now accelerate to get around the bend, and the water on the inside must slow down. This fast current does not simply change direction and continue downstream, however. Part of it hits the bank and dives downward along it, then spirals back along the bottom toward the inside of the bend. This motion of the current digs out the typical contour of a river bend: a deep pool on the outside and a shallow bar on the inside. Since there have been increases in both speed and volume of the current on the outside, that water has greater force and carrying capacity, increasing its potential to erode the bank. On the inside, however, the slower water begins to drop what it carried.

The result of this somewhat complicated interaction is that we expect to find deep, swift water, undercut rocks, exposed roots, and fallen trees on the outside of a river bend, and shallow bars of sand and debris on the inside. A paddler, too, will be pushed toward the outside of the bend unless he takes positive steps to prevent it.

If the bank is hard enough, however, the results are somewhat different. Although water will eventually erode even the hardest rock, over the short term a really unyielding bank cannot absorb significant energy through erosion. The energy of the river, in this case, rebounds back into the current, lifting the water into a noticeable hump or pillow along the wall. Add more current, and the hump becomes a wave. On really big rivers, this becomes a downstream-angled reaction wave several feet high coming off a canyon wall.

Water, like any fluid, will flow into the smallest space but cannot be compressed. This property has given rise to the whole science of hydraulics. Press on the brake pedal of your car and the pressure is transmitted directly to the brakes. Get air in the system, however, and you get a spongy feel on the brakes. Why? Air compresses, but brake fluid does not. The spongy feel is the air compressing before the transfer of pressure in the fluid can take place. Put enough air in the system, and it won't work at all. This principle also makes paddling possible. Wave your paddle in the air and nothing happens. Put it in the water and pull, and the boat moves. At the moment of your hardest pull, the water acts enough like a solid to let you pull the boat forward.

Later, we will speak of "squeezing" water, but it really can't be compressed like air. When flowing water is constricted, as when a river narrows, it must speed up. Confronted with an obstacle, like a boulder, it does not compress but, rather, piles up on the upstream side. When it then flows around the obstacle, it creates an *eddy* behind the obstacle. Since the water in the eddy downstream of the obstacle is lower than the water piled up in front of it, water flows back *up-*

stream toward the obstacle to fill in the resulting depression. This is one of the quirks of rivers that usually surprises the novice: we think of everything in a river flowing downstream, but even in the swiftest whitewater rivers there are strong upstream currents. In fact, there is a more or less direct proportion between the two currents: the swifter the downstream current, the swifter the upstream currents. These upstream currents constitute one of the major challenges of river running.

For a space behind the obstacle, the eddy and the main current flow adjacent to each other in opposite directions until the eddy finally loses strength and rejoins the downstream flow. This is the *eddy line*. In strong current there may be a marked height difference between the eddy and the downstream current, resulting in an *eddy fence*. In really big water an eddyline may be ten or more feet wide and laced with vortexes (commonly called swirlies) fully capable of upsetting a boat. These are caused by pieces of the eddy ripping away to join the stronger main current. Our river has now gained enough energy that its flow can no longer be described as laminar or helical. Swirlies are *turbulent* flow.

Let's go back for a moment to the white, frothy water piling up on the upstream side of an obstacle like a boulder. This is usually called a *cushion* or *pillow*, and it has the fortunate habit of pushing objects (like boats) away from the obstruction causing it. *If you don't see this pillow, beware.* The rock is probably undercut and is a potential pin site.

Obstructions and eddies are seldom found in isolation, however, and frequently the paddler must thread his way through a maze of boulders. Each boulder's upstream cushion sends a small shock wave out to the side at about a 45-degree angle downstream. If two boulders are close enough together, these small waves will intersect and form a V a short distance downstream of the rocks. The boulders will squeeze the water moving between them, so that it speeds up and rises into a smooth tongue of water. This *downstream V* is like a road sign on the interstate. Its unmarred face tells you of the smoothest, swiftest route downstream.

Then there are waves. Water's weight gives it consid-

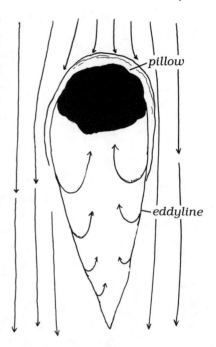

Anatomy of an eddy. A knowledge of eddies is essential for any activity involving moving water.

erable potential energy. A river, however, cannot store energy. When water speeds up, the river gains energy, which must then somehow be dissipated. The increase in speed usually comes in one of three ways. One is by compression, when the current is squeezed either horizontally into a narrow channel, or vertically by an obstruction on the bottom of the river. Another is when the river drops. There can also be a combination of both. A series of waves, gradually decreasing in height, can also dissipate this acquired energy. This is commonly called a *wave train*. If these waves are steep enough, they will break back upstream, forming an orderly white chain marching downstream. If there is a lot of energy, the tops of the waves will literally explode. On large rivers these wave trains are usually preceded by a smooth *tongue* of water that slides down over glass-smooth waves until the current gains enough energy to make the waves break. John Wesley Powell, in his classic *The Exploration of the Colorado River and Its Canyons*, described it thus: "The waters plunge down ten or twenty feet to the foot of a fall, spring up again in a great wave, then down and up in a series of billows that gradually disappear . . . "

River waves, unlike ocean waves, stand in one place. The reason is that on a river, the water moves over a fixed obstacle, dissipating its energy. On a large body of still water (the ocean or a big lake), however, the water stays more or less stationary while the energy imparted to it, usually by the wind, traverses it in the form of moving waves.

On shallow, rocky rivers, look for the main current, since this is usually where the deepest water lies. The route is often marked by a series of waves. On a gentle flatwater stream, these may be mere riffles, but on a river like the Niagara they may be twenty feet high. To the novice paddler, the white train of waves marking the main current and the white cushions on the upstream side of boulders look much the same. The key is to recognize a pattern. Although boulders are generally scattered at random, wave trains tend to occur in regular series. If there is a break in the pattern, it's usually caused by a rock.

So far we have looked only at water that flows around obstacles. Water that flows over an obstacle first rises into a cushion, then accelerates as it drops over the obstacle, gaining enough energy thereby to create a wave a little distance downstream. Between the obstacle and the downstream wave is a depression, or *hole*, into which water flows. As with an eddy, this creates an upstream current (holes are sometimes called vertical eddies). Unlike an eddy, however, a hole can be extremely dangerous, since it may sometimes hold a buoyant object for an extended period of time. That could be you! It does this in two ways. First, the force of gravity *pulls* the boat down into the depression in the water, forcing it to move uphill to escape. Second, the backwash *pushes* a boat back upstream into the hole. If conditions are right, the backwash may develop into a vertically recirculating current, called a *hydraulic*, which is particularly dangerous for a boat or swimmer. A person caught in a hydraulic will be pushed underwater by the water flowing over the obstacle, pulled along the bottom by the accelerating downstream current, then pop up to the surface, only to be pulled back toward the drop by the backwash flowing upstream. The more regular the obstacle that creates the hydraulic, the harder it is to escape. Man-made dams and weirs are particularly dangerous, since they frequently form a regular hydraulic all the way across the river. These drowning machines often do not look bad at all. Some of the worst ones are gentle, sloping drops of only a few feet.

One of the vaguest areas of river terminology centers on exactly what holes are. You will see them referred to as souse-holes, pour-overs, and many other names. For the sake of consistency, we will refer to any river feature with an upstream-flowing current (other than an eddy) as a *hydraulic*, and anything else (generally a depression followed by a breaking wave) as a *hole*.

TIP: To identify a hydraulic, look for the white foamy water moving upstream back into the drop that created it. At a certain point below the drop there is an upsurge of water, called the boil line, where water appears to be boiling up from under the surface. About half of this water goes back into the hydraulic, and the other half, which has a somewhat darker appearance, flows downstream.

Now imagine more water flowing over that rock or boulder. As the volume of water increases, the depth of the water flowing over the submerged rock also increases. There is a pile of water upstream of the boulder. As it flows over the top of the boulder, gravity causes it to accelerate. This results in a gain of energy, and to dissipate this acquired energy, the size of the downstream wave becomes larger.

At a certain point (when the height of the wave equals one seventh of the distance from crest to crest) this wave begins to break back upstream. By the time the water is deep enough for this to happen, the re-circulating current of the hydraulic has stopped, al-

An undercut rock does not form an upstream pillow.

An obstacle in the river such as a rock forms a pillow upstream and an eddy downstream.

When the water flows over the obstacle, a hydraulic forms just downstream of the rock, with a backwash flowing upstream.

As the water deepens, it forms a wave or wave/hole behind the obstacle breaking upstream.

Deep underwater the obstacle is marked only by a series of small waves.

though the force of the wave breaking back upstream often has a similar holding effect on boats. The foaming crest of the wave breaking upstream is characteristic of this feature, and this type of hole is often called a *breaking hole*. As the water over our hypothetical boulder deepens, the angle of the wave becomes less steep and it ceases to break (often becoming an excellent surfing wave in the process), then turns into a standing wave. As the water becomes deeper yet, the wave shrinks to a small hump on the surface, and finally, with the boulder deeply buried underwater, it disappears altogether.

It's easy to see how rapids and sections of river can change dramatically with the river's water level.

HAZARDS. There are hazards on rivers, just as there are on highways. Even though we are only seconds away from potential death or injury when moving on the highway at normal speeds, we take those dangers lightly because they are familiar. We avoid perils like slick spots on the pavement, inspect our tires and brakes so that they don't fail when we need them, slow down in the rain, and so on. Likewise, paddling entails learning to uncover the dangers a river holds.

For instance, we have seen how water forms a cushion on the upstream side of most obstacles. But not all of them. A rounded boulder wears an upstream cushion where the water hits the upstream face, but if the rock into which the water flows is *undercut*, water will flow underneath it. Consequently, there will be little or no cushion on the upstream side of the rock. This presents a twofold disadvantage. Since there is nothing to push a boat away from the undercut, it is very easy for the boat to be driven against the rock and held there by the current. Worse, when this happens, the boat is often forced under the rock—a place from which rescue or recovery is difficult. Undercuts are more frequent on geologically older rivers, such as those found in the Appalachians. On geologically younger rivers, such as those in the Sierras, a comparable hazard is the *boulder sieve*, usually formed by the outwash of boulders from a side creek during a flash flood. Boulder sieves can entrap both boats and people.

Another common, and often deadly, hazard is the *strainer*. This is usually a tree or log that has become lodged across the current. Unlike most other obstructions, a strainer allows water to flow right through it, but not solid objects, like people and boats. Often strainers are difficult to see, and on narrow rivers they can block the entire channel. A strainer often appears on the outside of a bend; water erodes the soil from the root system, felling the tree into the river. A strainer can often hide just beneath the surface, its presence only hinted at by a small ripple of water. A person or a boat swept into a strainer will be swept against the branches and often be unable to escape.

Rivers that have been used for logging or industry, or simply for dumping waste, may hold all sorts of hazards, from steel reinforcing rods to barrels, junk cars, and even industrial conveyor belts, which may snag or impale a boater. Bridge pilings also deserve special mention, since these man-made structures provide almost no water cushion to keep river traffic clear of them.

Finally, there is the danger of cold water. "Cold" is a relative term, and even relatively warm water (as warm as 70°F) sucks heat out of a paddler's body at an alarming rate—some twenty-five times as fast as air of the same temperature. Although few paddlers actually die of hypothermia, it is very often a contributing factor in drownings. Acute, or immersion, hypothermia can quickly reduce a swimmer's strength and coordination, complicating the rescue. This problem is more likely on big, wide rivers, where immersion is likely to be prolonged.

We'll talk more about hazards—and what to do about them—in chapters 6 and 10.

THE BEHAVIOR OF RIVERS. In some ways rivers are like people, and to some extent their behavior can be predicted by their appearance: a man in a business suit usually acts differently than one in overalls. A gentle meandering stream, for example, will be quite predictable. We can make some generalizations. If the river widens, its energy spreads and dissipates, and usually it becomes slower and shallower, having less power to cut into its bed. A very deep river will be calm, even though the current may be swift. But when we have shallow water and the river narrows, there is generally some kind of reaction, some sort of energy to be given up, particularly if there is a drop in elevation.

As with people, however, appearances can be deceptive: the man in a business suit may be a farmer in his Sunday best, and the man in overalls may be a stockbroker gardening on his day off. Likewise, our meandering stream may cross a geologic boundary and begin dropping suddenly. (Be observant at places of obvious geologic change.) Paddlers on almost any river may encounter a low-head dam or weir, which can turn even a mild-mannered stream into a killer. Both low-head dams and steep rapids have one common feature that every paddler should learn to identify early on: the horizon line. Normally you can see quite a ways downriver—at least to the next bend. If all you see is a featureless line across the river and nothing below it, the river has dropped abruptly. It's time to get off the water for a look.

Or our gentle stream may be in flood, in which case it is no longer gentle. Continuing our analogy with people, our mild-mannered stockbroker has snapped and is now a crazed gunman, capable of anything. Let's look at a few reasons you might want to stay off flooded rivers. First, when you put a lot of water into a riverbed that normally carries only a little, the water speeds up dramatically. Current speeds of over fifteen miles per hour are not unheard of, and things happen a lot faster than you are probably accustomed to. Second, depending on the size of its bed, the river may spread out, flowing into the trees. Each tree is a potential strainer, and the simple act of pulling over to the bank can be extremely dangerous. Third, there is often a great deal of debris in the water (remember the increase in carrying capacity), eddylines become vicious and unpredictable, and the main current now operates more by the laws of ballistics than by the principles of hydraulics. The helical currents near shore now assume major proportions and tend to sweep both boats and swimmers back into the main current. This makes rescue, including self-rescue, very difficult. As a general rule, consider a river to be in flood when it comes up out of its banks and stay off it.

Basic Route Finding

We now know the what and why of basic river features and the hazards to avoid, so it's time to start thinking about where to go. Before we do this, let's define a few more terms. When describing the location of river features, we use the terms *river right* and *river left*. These refer to the right and left sides of the river as we are looking *downstream*. We will cover river tactics in more detail later in chapter 6, but for now let's look at the basic path a boat will follow down a river.

Consider a simple section of river first, one you might find almost anywhere. To determine where to go, follow these simple steps: find the deepest, widest, least obstructed channel through the rapid. Now trace it all the way through the rapid, connecting the dots. That's the route. Look for any hazards or other dangers that might make you want to go elsewhere. Riverboatmen in Twain's day did it no differently. The practice of looking at a section of river before running it is called *scouting*. If you can see all the way down the section, you may scout it from your boat. Otherwise, it's good idea to get out on the bank and take a look at

A hypothetical rapid. Water piles up on the front of obstacles and forms eddies behind them. The current forms downstream-pointing Vs between obstacles, and this generally indicates the best route past them. Standing waves usually form at the end of the tongue. Submerged rocks form holes.

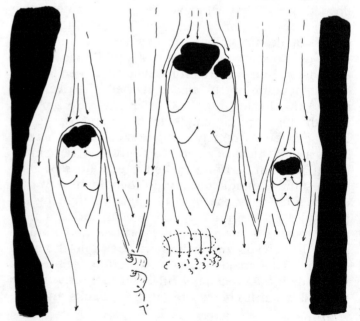

After Jan Atlee © 1990

anything you can't see. Even a section you've run a hundred times may have a tree across it after a recent thunderstorm.

In the rapid shown opposite, water flowing between the boulders forms a downstream V, which we know to be the deepest channel. The tongue is smooth, indicating there are no rocks near the surface. This is where we will go. Below that are a series of small standing waves. They are too small to swamp us, and they form a regular pattern, so we know that these are waves and not submerged rocks or holes. Ah, but what's that off to the side? Another patch of white! It doesn't fit into the regular pattern of the waves, so let's walk down and take a closer look. There is a small hump with water flowing over it. Behind it is frothy water moving back upstream. This is a hydraulic, and although it's a small one, we will avoid it by staying on the river-right side of the wave train.

TIP: *To find your way through runnable waves:*
* *Stay in the wave series—the water is deepest there.*
* *If you see a feature off by itself, like a single wave—avoid it. There's probably a rock just upstream of it. Experience will eventually tell you whether you can float over it or not.*
* *Flat or calm places amid turbulence are either eddies or hydraulics. How lucky do you feel?*
* *Look for where the water is going in and coming out.*

—Dave Moccia

That was simple enough. Now let's apply these same principles to look at another, more complex situation. The river illustrated on the next page has a rapid, or several, depending on how you look at it. At first glance the picture seems chaotic, but soon discernible patterns emerge from the crashing water.

Before the rapid, where the water backs up above it, is a calm pool. This slow current makes it an easy place to pull over and scout. At the top of the rapid **A** there is an almost river-wide ledge with a break on the river-right side. From upstream all we can see is a horizon line across the river (another reason to scout),

Route finding through a
typical rapid.

After Jan Atlee © 1990

with the right side of the line slightly lower. After walking down to look at it, we see that this ledge forms a
hydraulic. Below the ledge, we can see foaming water
moving back upstream. On the river right is a smooth
tongue of water forming a downstream V between a
boulder and the ledge. Here, then, is the path.

What's downstream? If we break this long rapid up
into sections, it will be easier to analyze and, later, to
run. Below the ledge is a hole **B**, probably caused by a
submerged boulder, and beside it **C** is another boulder with an eddy behind. Between the two obstacles is
a downstream V, indicating a clear path. This V is

more or less in a direct line with the one above it, which would make for a straight shot through both of these features. But this path, though clear, leads straight into a hazard: a strainer.

The water scouring the outside of the riverbank has undercut the roots of a large tree, felling it into the river. Much of the river's main current goes right through it, and avoiding it will require an abrupt turn. Looking back at the boulder, we see that there is another, smaller V on the river-right side of the boulder. Though not as straight a path, it avoids the strainer and puts us in a much better position to negotiate the upcoming bend. Also, as mentioned before, it's a good idea to stay toward the inside of a bend.

Looking farther down, we see that even if the tree were not there, there is an undercut rock **D** to avoid. Across from the undercut rock is an eddy **E**. The main current flows between the two, and to stay on the inside of the bend, we want to hug the eddyline while staying in the main flow.

Below that sits a boulder garden **F** and a series of standing waves **G** where the river narrows and drops a bit. Here we can't hug the inside of the bend as we did upstream because that would put us into the boulder garden. So we must skirt the boulder garden on the right, staying as far left in the current as we can without hitting the rocks, and head for the big waves at the bottom of the chute. The path is clear, but whether we run waves, skirt them, or portage them depends on their size (as well as our skill level and the type of boat we are in). If there is a long, calm pool at the end of the rapid, we may chance it, knowing that there is plenty of room to recover from a spill.

Now that we understand the basic fluid mechanics of the river, it's time to consider our part in this picture. All this movement and power in the river affects boats, sometimes dramatically. Even a small river can rip a boat apart and pummel or drown a paddler. It is useless—and needless—to resist or attempt to overpower a river. Paddlers, unlike the misguided souls who build dams, use the power of the river to their advantage. There are places, as we saw above, where the river gains and then gives up a tremendous

Rivers and Boats

A SAMPLE RIVER

Depth times width times current velocity equals the river's flow in cubic units (feet or meters) per second—that is, the number of cubic units of water that pass a given point on the bank in one second.

Let's take a hypothetical river and see what happens when we change things around. Our river has a width of 10 feet and a depth of 10 feet. Let's make the bed and banks straight and smooth. The current velocity is 6 feet per second. Multiplying the width times the depth times the current velocity ($10 \times 10 \times 6$) gives a water volume of 600 cubic feet per second. This current would push against a person's body with a force of about 134 pounds. Against a pinned boat it will be about 672 pounds.

Now let's have a flooded tributary dump in an additional 300 cfs for a total of 900 cfs. Since the width and depth remain constant, the velocity increases in linear fashion to 9 feet per second. But the force, increasing as the cube, jumps to 302 pounds on a person's body and 1,512 pounds on a pinned boat.

As the river gets a little shallower—let's say its depth is now only 7½ feet—while the volume remains the same, the current speed picks up to 12 feet per second ($900/10 \times 7.5 = 12$). The force now jumps to 538 pounds on a body and 2,688 on a pinned boat.

amount of energy. Depending on the type of paddling you do and the situation, you may choose either to avoid this power or to make it your own. Many forces act upon a boat in the river, but here we need to consider only the two most basic: capsizing forces and rotational forces.

Once a boat enters the river, it quickly accelerates to the speed of the current. Without other contending forces, like waves, the current has little direct effect on the boat if both are moving at the same speed. The paddler may move forward, backward, and from side to side even in a swiftly moving current much as if he were on a lake. The problems begin when current differentials appear—when the speed of the boat does not match that of the current. And the current differentials can be considerable. Even on a slow stream with a two-mile-per-hour current, the difference between an eddyline and the main current can be almost double that, or three to four miles per hour (the upstream speed of an eddy current is not quite as high as the downstream speed of the main current). On whitewater rivers it may be extremely high.

The effect of this current differential is to pull the rug out from under the paddler. Let's take an example: a boat pulling out of an eddy into the main current. The water in the eddy is flowing upstream, separated from the main current by the eddyline. This means the boat is either still or moving slightly upstream. When a boat crosses the eddyline, it presents its side to a current moving in the opposite direction. As it does, the force of the current quite suddenly drives against the bottom of the boat. Even in a relatively mild three-mile-per-hour current this can amount to thirty to fifty foot-pounds of *capsizing force* abruptly trying to roll the boat over *upstream*. The same situation exists when the boat comes out of the main current into an eddy. Obviously the paddler must apply some kind of counterforce or the boat will flip upstream and he will get a chilly reminder of the river's power. In the next chapter we'll see just how he'll do this.

Now let's rewind and look at this again, for there is also a *rotational force* that causes the boat to turn around when it crosses the eddyline. If the boat is in the eddy and crosses into the main current, the cur-

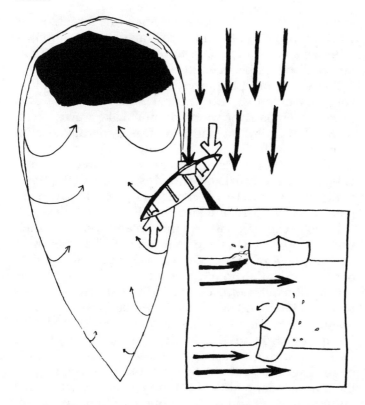

The forces acting on a canoe in a peel-out or eddy turn. The eddy current pushes the boat upstream while the main current pushes the boat downstream. This horizontal force (white arrows) tends to spin the boat around on the eddy line. The vertical component (dark arrows) tries to overturn the boat by pushing on the bottom. When the boat is halfway across the eddy line, as here, these forces cancel each other. As the boat moves into or out of the eddy, however, the vertical forces increase until the boat's speed matches the speed of the current. Upsetting force on the hull of a canoe (inset). As the canoe pulls out into the current, water piles up on the upstream side (top) and attempts to rotate the boat upstream. Unless the paddler applies a counter-lean, this usually results in a flip (bottom).

rent begins to push the bow of the boat downstream from the moment it crosses the eddyline. The more of the boat that crosses the eddyline, the greater the push. The stern of the boat, still in the eddy, continues to move upstream, with the result that the boat rotates downstream without any action from the paddler. It is the same when entering an eddy: as the boat crosses from the main current into the eddy, the bow enters the upstream current in the eddy and begins to turn upstream. The more of the bow that enters the eddy, the more the boat turns as the downstream current continues to push the stern around. This is the basis of two important river maneuvers: the eddy turn and the peel-out.

The other primary force operating on water is the wind. On rivers, gravity is by far the stronger force, and wind merely a nuisance, but on lakes the situation is reversed. Although very large lakes have tides like the ocean, for the most part the role of gravity is to

Wind

keep lakes flat. A lake does present a fine target for the wind, whose effect is similar to gravity in that it makes otherwise flat water stand up. There are some important differences between these two types of waves.

The waves on a big lake can be as big as anything you'll see on a river. But these wind-driven lake waves move, whereas river waves do not. Lake waves break when they grow too tall, but this generally occurs when the water becomes shallower near the shore, causing the familiar shore break. A stiff breeze causes chop—a small break off the tops of the waves—and really large waves may have their tops blown completely off by hurricane-force winds.

Much of the effect of the wind depends on how much water it touches. On the ocean or a big lake, there may be hundreds of miles of open water for the wind to operate on, so although it is not as great a force as gravity, it can become considerable. Cut the winds, as behind a headland or in a sheltered bay, and the waves abate. In general, the biggest waves on a lake are found on the leeward end, that is, the end against which the wind has the greatest distance to gather force (this open length is called the *fetch*). In areas having predictable winds, paddlers can stay near the windward end of the lake, and on more open sections use headlands and islands for cover.

However, not all winds are predictable. For paddlers, much of the danger of lake paddling comes from swamping or capsizing too far away from shore for self-rescue. In cold water, this may not be as far away as you think. The Coast Guard reports that a majority of lake and ocean drownings take place within one hundred yards of shore. Thunderstorms can come up suddenly, bringing blinding rain and gale-force winds to what was a calm pond. Swiftly moving weather fronts can have similar effects. For lake paddlers, weather reading is as important as water reading is to the river paddler. Learn to read the weather or stay near shore.

TWO

Preparation
for Paddling

THERE IS A CERTAIN undeniable mystique about paddling, an indefinable point where boat and paddler become one, whether it be on a serene, misty river in
Georgia or in the frothy backwash of a whitewater river
in California. So far, you must accept my assurance
that such a point exists. Finding it may involve long
hours, frustration, and endless practice, but if you per-
severe, you will attain it. It requires preparation, both
mental and physical, and knowledge, as well as a vision of what you will achieve. But here, at the beginning, we must concern ourselves with foundations.
Like any other sport, paddling has its fundamentals:
the bedrock upon which the bricks of skill are laid.

The three parts of this foundation are these:
• Body movement and balance
• The placement of the paddle in the water
• The place of the boat on the river.

In this chapter and the next we will be primarily
concerned with the first two. We have already briefly
covered the basics of the river and will deal more fully
with the interaction of boat, paddler, and water in
chapter 4. There are many technical things to learn,
but first, let's look at ourselves. Before we even get into

a boat, what can we do to make paddling easier and to help our skills develop faster?

Preparation

Make the commitment to approach paddling as a *sport*. Yes, you can get into a rental canoe and float down the river on a summer's day. It's very enjoyable, and many people are happy to go no further than that. Or you may learn to cheat, to pick up little tricks to get you by, like sliding out of the back of an eddy instead of peeling out. But in neither case, if your true goal is to paddle, will you be satisfied, nor is there any real reason for you to read this book. Don't be afraid of the word *sport*. Almost any kind of physical fitness activity is a sport. It doesn't necessarily mean heavy workouts and a competitive atmosphere, nor does it mean you have to be a twenty-year-old jock. But you will need to prepare, or you will hurt.

"Okay," you say. "I'm not an athlete or a racer. I just want to paddle and I don't care about maximum efficiency." Fine, but look at it this way. A racer needs that efficiency so that his highly trained body can push the boat just a little faster than the next guy's. *You* need it so that you can paddle, because increased efficiency equals more control with less work. Get the picture?

Think for a minute about your car. If you're going on a long cross-country trip, you check out the car and get it tuned up. On the water, you are the engine that propels the canoe, and you should be in a reasonable state of tune. You owe your body the same courtesy as your car, but the mechanic here is your doctor. As any instructor will tell you, it's not unusual at canoe clinics to have people show up who have lifted nothing heavier than a can of Bud in the last twelve months. Do you believe in magic? If not, keep reading.

First, are you in halfway decent physical shape? Do you smoke? Are you winded after climbing a flight of stairs? Do you have any physical limitations? Most physical limitations can be overcome or compensated for, but only if you are aware of them.

Second, are you comfortable in the water? Swimming ability *per se* is not as important as being able to resist panic when finding yourself unexpectedly in the drink. However, do not think that because you are a strong swimmer you are automatically ready for white water. Swimming ability certainly helps, but the rules are different in a swiftly flowing river.

Third, do you participate in any other sports? Jog or run regularly? Play any sports involving upper-body exercise, like racquetball, tennis, or weight lifting? Canoeing is an exercise sport, even on flat water. In fact, it is an even more exercise-intensive sport on totally flat water, since there is no current from which to borrow energy. If you lead the sedentary life of a couch potato, especially if you are over forty, get a physical exam. Begin your physical fitness program gradually. The first few days of a canoe clinic are likely to be frustrating enough without discovering that out-of-work muscles are reluctant to take up the task again. Muscles that have not been used regularly, or since last season, protest by failing early and being sore the next day. And soreness interferes with learning. As a general rule, if you are able to play an afternoon's game of softball or touch football without ill effects the next day, you will do fine. Endurance and coordination are more important in paddling than is brute strength.

Running, bicycling, cross-country skiing, and similar sports all build the endurance needed for paddling but don't do much for upper-body strength. An upper-body weight program that emphasizes repetitions rather than heavy lifts, combined with a stretching program, can be very beneficial. And even the strongest, most toned muscles must be warmed up and stretched before use, just as your car should be warmed up on a cold morning before driving. The best way to do this is with a simple stretching program.

Stretching and Warm-up Exercises

Stretching not only warms up your muscles, it also increases body flexibility. This is especially true of the big muscles of the trunk, which play a large part in canoeing. Body flexibility is desirable in any sport, but particularly so in canoeing. Some strokes, especially cross and reverse strokes, require considerable flexibility. Paddling requires a certain amount of finesse, and a supple, flexible body is more adaptable to its demands than a stiff but strong one. Increasing your flexibility, extension, and range of motion will enable you to put the paddle in the water farther forward and

carry it through a greater range. This leads to better overall technique and a greater enjoyment of paddling. As you continue, you'll see how flexibility fits in with paddle strokes and the fundamentals of canoeing. For now, however, take it on faith that you want to achieve the following goals:

• To rotate your torso up to 90 degrees on both sides.

• To be loose enough in your quadriceps (the big muscle on the front of the thigh) and ankles to kneel comfortably.

• To have enough upper-body flexibility to be able to extend the paddle fully and move it through a full range of motion for each stroke.

• To have enough overall flexibility to use your body and head to balance and counterbalance the canoe.

Like paddling itself, stretching must be practiced to be effective, and works best when combined with a regular exercise program. Stretch before and after exercise, as well as before and after paddling. Stretching exercises warm muscles gently and slowly, and this helps prevent injury. One really important area to warm up is your lower back—before lifting the canoe. Ideally, you should begin a stretching program lasting twenty to thirty minutes, once or twice a day, at least a couple of weeks prior to the start of paddling. Work into it gradually, and don't expect overnight results. However, if you are faithful to your program, you *will* see—and feel—a difference.

If you're over forty, or if you work in an office or lead a sedentary life, stretching becomes even more important not just for canoeing, but for your general lifestyle. We lose body flexibility as we get older—or if we don't exercise. Buy a book and learn about it. The standard reference on the subject is Bob Anderson's *Stretching* (see the Resources section), a book that should inhabit every paddler's library. Anderson's book has stretches you can do even in an office.

Now that you're convinced, start with a simple program, such as the following one, developed by the Nantahala Outdoor Center as a preclinic warm-up for all types of paddlers. If you follow it regularly over a period of weeks, it will lead to greater comfort and efficiency while paddling. But don't stop there: keep

Neck, upper back, shoulders   doing it until your flexibility really increases.

This set of exercises, designed for the out-of-shape, loosen and warm the areas of your body used in boating. It also works well as a prepaddling warm-up. Greater flexibility will allow you to move the boat through the water much more easily.

Some stretches will be easier than others. Do *not* force these exercises. While stretching, breathe regularly and deeply, relaxing your shoulders and neck. Hold each position for about ten seconds. *Do not bounce.* Bouncing contracts and tightens muscles and can lead to painful muscle tears. If you have a history of lower-back or knee problems, or if you have any doubts about how much stretching you should do, consult your doctor.

FOR NECK, UPPER BACK, AND SHOULDERS.

1. Stand straight with your shoulders and neck relaxed. Using only your head and shoulders, slowly alternate dropping your head forward and back. Next drop your ear toward your shoulder on each side, moving only your head and neck. Hold each position for ten seconds. Repeat twice.

2. Keeping your lower back straight, repeat the first sequence while bending at the waist. Lead with your head.

FOR TRUNK ROTATION.

1. Look over your right shoulder as far as possible, then over the left shoulder. Turn only your head and neck, not your torso. Hold each position for ten seconds. Repeat twice.

2. Repeat the above stretch, but this time use your shoulders also. Rotate the trunk of your body down to the waist. Your goal is to turn your shoulders in a straight line 90 degrees to the direction in which your feet are pointing.

FOR TORSO AND LOWER BACK.

Avoid straight-leg sit-ups, which can cause strains. Instead, try the following exercise to strengthen the abdominal muscles:

1. Lie on your back with your knees bent and flat on the floor. Place your hands loosely on your chest. With your chin tilted down toward your chest, lift your shoulder blades, curling forward to an angle of about 30 degrees. Be sure to keep your lower back flat on the floor. Then relax. Do several of these at a medium speed.

Trunk rotation

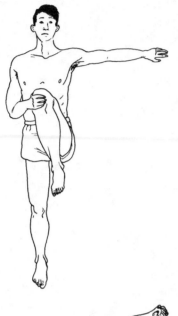

2. Lie on your back with your arms outstretched at shoulder level, palms down. Keep your right leg straight and bend your left knee up toward your chest. Using your right hand, bring the left knee across your torso. Keep your left shoulder in contact with the floor. Relax, letting the weight of your thigh and hand bring the knee closer to the floor. Hold for one minute. Repeat for the other side.

3. Stand with your feet two to two and a half feet apart, toes turned out. Clasp your hands overhead with your arms straight. Bend your upper body to the right, being careful not to twist sideways. Hold this position for ten seconds, then repeat for the left side. Do both sides twice.

FOR HIP JOINTS AND BACKS OF LEGS.

1. With your weight on the balls of your feet and knees slightly bent, bend over and place your hands either on the floor or on a stool of comfortable height. Your upper body should rest against your thighs and your face should be close to your knees. Now gradually straighten your legs and concentrate on increased flexion of the upper thighs. It is not important to keep your hands on the floor: the idea is to flex at the hip as your legs straighten.

2. Sit on the floor with your legs together and your back straight. Now reach forward toward your toes while keeping your back straight. Feel the stretch in your upper and lower legs.

Torso and lower back

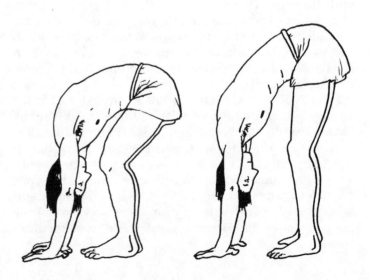

Hip joints

Hamstrings

Hamstrings

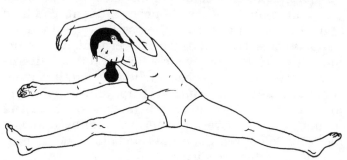

3. Sit up and open your legs as far as possible. Drop your left shoulder toward your left knee. Relax and hold. Now drop your head toward the floor in front of you. Relax and hold. Follow the same routine to the right, then repeat the entire sequence.

A word or two about instruction programs and skill levels is appropriate here, since both affect your rate of learning. There are three ways to learn canoeing (and paddling in general):

Instruction Programs

• From a course or clinic with a paid professional organization like the Nantahala Outdoor Center.

• From a volunteer organization like a club or university outing program.

• From friends.

The first way is probably the best and fastest, but it is also the most expensive. The instructors will be expert paddlers themselves *and* they will know how to *teach* canoeing. Many experts are poor instructors, which is why learning from friends, no matter how good they might be, can be frustrating. Although the course of instruction is free, friends frequently put their own enjoyment of the river before teaching.

A good middle ground is a paddling club. Many clubs have excellent instruction programs for all phases of paddling, available for only the price of club dues. Ask whether the instructors are certified by the American Canoe Association. Though this does not absolutely guarantee expert instruction, it is a start.

Finally, you can teach yourself from books and videos, but these usually are best used to reinforce and sharpen your skills.

Before taking any course of instruction, first evaluate your skill level. Be honest. Student paddlers almost universally overrate their skill level, something that has caused a great deal of concern among instructors. By overestimating your skill level you do a disservice to everyone, but especially to yourself. If you are constantly straining just to keep up, you are not learning and may be holding up others who could be. And finally, you will have a greater sense of accomplishment by doing well in an intermediate clinic than by barely surviving an advanced one.

Think of learning as a dynamic tension between the *challenge*, loosely defined as the difficulty of performing a skill, and your *ability*. There are four phases:

• Phase I: Ability is greater than challenge. The result is boredom.

• Phase II: Ability is equal to challenge. The result is fun, but this tends to slide into boredom after a while.

• Phase III: Challenge is *somewhat* greater than ability. This is where you learn the most. You are challenged to learn, but not overwhelmed or frightened. As a general guideline, if you are able to make a required move somewhere between 50 percent and 75 percent of the time, you're in the ballpark.

• Phase IV: Challenge is *much* greater than ability. If you're making a required move less than half the time, you are definitely in this category. Though it is possible to learn here, the most normal results are fear and frustration. The cure is to drop back one level.

Evaluate yourself realistically. You can start by using these simple guidelines, developed by the Nantahala Outdoor Center for their clinic system.

Beginners:
• Have never paddled a boat before.
• Have paddled fewer than five times on white water.
• Are not comfortable with boat leans without grabbing the gunnels.

Beginner–intermediates:
• Paddle in a straight line without problems.
• Execute and understand concepts of basic ferries, peel-outs, and eddy turns.
• Have paddled five to ten times on white water.

Intermediates:
• Have paddled on Class II water more than ten times.
• Perform eddy turns and peel-outs on Class II.
• Can control ferry angle in swift Class II current.
• Can accelerate the boat across eddylines.
• Surf small waves and holes.
• Are comfortable with self-rescue on Class II.

Advanced paddlers:
• Perform eddy turns, peel-outs, and ferries with confidence on Class III water.
• Have strong high and low braces and paddle aggressively.
• Assist with rescues.
• Catch one to two boat eddies on Class III water.

If you're unsure what any of these terms mean, start at the beginning. Obviously these are very general categories. If you're still not sure, consider these further guidelines for borderline cases.

Take a lower-level course if you:
• Have paddled few rivers repeatedly.
• Exercise once a week (or not at all).
• Are a bit wary or tentative.

- Are rusty or prefer to sit in the eddies and watch.
- Have had fewer than three days of formal instruction.

Take a higher-level course if you:
- Have paddled a wide variety of rivers.
- Are engaged in a regular fitness program or exercise more than twice a week.
- Are confident or aggressive, and are willing to jump in and play.
- Have had more than three days of formal instruction.

The Five Fundamentals of Paddling

THE PADDLER'S BOX
To gain maximum power and reduce the chance of injury, a paddler should keep his hands inside an imaginary box. This box stays in front of the paddler's upper *body*, not the boat. The gunnels form the bottom, and the top of the paddler's head marks the top. The front of the box is as far forward as he can reach, and the back of the box is the plane of the paddler's shoulders. The box's sides are the width of the paddler's normal grip. To keep his hands in the box, the paddler must rotate his body when making a stroke on either side—exactly what we want.

Enough preparation. Let's talk about paddling! The fundamental tenets of paddling have been distilled into five areas by Billy Richards, a Nantahala kayak instructor, but they are applicable to almost any boat or paddling situation. They also give us an insight into the nature of the sport, and will figure in one way or the other in almost everything we do on the river.

FIRST FUNDAMENTAL. *Posture.* Sit up straight. Paddling is a balance sport, depending much more on equilibrium and finesse than on muscle. Your waist is a hinge that flexes forward and back and from side to side. This hinge works much better with your body sitting straight. Sit up and see how much easier it is to move from side to side, and to rotate your shoulders back and forth. Now lean forward, as a lot of paddlers do, and try it again. Notice the difference. This simple principle makes balancing the boat much easier.

SECOND FUNDAMENTAL. *Keep your body weight over the boat.* This acts in concert with the First Fundamental to further assist in balancing the boat. You will hear some people telling you to lean out over the gunnel and put your weight on the paddle blade in a brace. Not only can the blade not support much weight, but while bracing it can't be used for anything more constructive—like powering the boat. Paddles are better used for propulsion than for support. If you think you can put your weight on the paddle, suggests Professor Richards, get astride it and try riding it down a rapid. A canoeist adjusts his weight in the boat by shifting it to one knee, tilting the boat up on one side while keeping his body over the boat. A novice canoeist, on the other hand, does almost exactly the opposite, keeping the hull flat (because it feels more stable) and leaning his body out over the water, bracing with his paddle if necessary. This ruins the balance of the canoe and makes it easier to catch the edge when crossing currents. Weight shifts and balance, although seldom emphasized in paddling literature (which tends to concentrate on the mysteries of strokes) are every bit as important as artistry with a blade.

THIRD FUNDAMENTAL. *The boat moves, not the paddle.* Otherwise, how would you get anywhere? Think of the paddle as set in concrete. The paddler reaches forward, plants the paddle in the concrete and *pulls the boat forward.* Some instructors consider this the single most important principle of paddling.

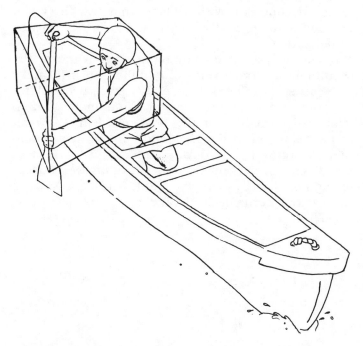

The paddler's box is an imaginary square in front of the paddler. By keeping his hands in the box, the paddler reduces his chances of injury and increases the power of his strokes. In order to keep his hands in the box, the paddler must rotate his body when taking strokes over the side of the boat.

VISUALIZATION

Instinct encourages us to search for the easiest way to learn a new skill. The easy way to learning whitewater canoeing sometimes seems to be evasive. "You aren't learning unless you swim" is a typical well-intended comment to dripping wet, freezing paddlers just after a swim. But visualization, a sort of deliberate daydreaming, can be a shortcut in the learning process.

Visualize exactly how you will run a rapid. Do you finish it upside down? Then create a new daydream, this time with a confident dry finish. Remember the time you were successful at a similar rapid. Or superimpose the image of yourself in the boat of a successful paddler (videos of good paddlers can help). Practice visualizations from several different points of view. Watch an image of yourself running the rapid well. Then imagine yourself walking upstream to your boat, climbing in, reviewing your landmarks and feeling confident. Feel the boat responding to every stroke and current in the water. Hear the roar of the rapids around you. Put your boat right where you want it, and finish the run, ecstatic.

—*Kent Ford*

FOURTH FUNDAMENTAL. *The body turns with the paddle blade.* Body rotation is a key element of paddling for two reasons. First, the arms are really only connectors to the real source of power—the torso. The rotation of the torso around the spine provides much more power for all strokes than does the push-pull motion of the arms. Second, body rotation reduces the chances of a shoulder injury, which often happens when the upper arm gets behind the plane of the shoulders and then is moved forcefully away from the body. Keep your hands inside the paddler's box.

FIFTH FUNDAMENTAL. *Vision.* The farther you look in front of the boat, the better paddler you will be. Beginners seldom look beyond the grab loop, intermediates to the first rock, advanced paddlers to the next drop, and experts downstream through an entire rapid. Work to expand your vision, for it is this, as much as your skill with a blade, that will carry you through a rapid or down a river. Vision also means visualization.

Once you learn these fundamentals, some of the seemingly arbitrary rules of paddling start to make more sense. When you do an eddy turn or peel-out, for instance, think of the Second Fundamental—keep your body weight over the boat and lean the boat rather than your body. The Third and Fourth Fundamentals apply to almost any stroke, and the Fifth is one we can all work on. By understanding the concept of paddling as a system, you will learn faster. Now it's time to look at the heart of paddling: the strokes.

THREE

Basic Strokes

IN 1983 the American Canoe Association and the American Red Cross adopted a common set of paddling terms to reduce confusion in the paddling community. We will review them quickly, beginning with the language and terms adopted by the ACA's National Instruction Committee. Our concern will be the similarities among strokes rather than the differences; as the ACA's *Instruction Manual* correctly declares, all strokes "are based on the same principles of motion." Various boat designs may make any of these strokes harder or easier, but the principles remain the same. The ACA, in its *Instruction Manual*, recognizes three basic types of strokes:

• *Power.* These strokes provide forward or reverse momentum.

• *Turning or corrective.* These strokes turn the boat so that it veers from a straight course or is brought back onto a straight course.

• *Braces.* Their primary function is to provide stability for the craft, although they can also help the boat turn.

The ACA further classifies each stroke as *on-side*, if executed on the selected paddling side, and *cross*, or *off-side*, when executed on the other side of the canoe without your switching hands. The subject of canoe paddles is a rich one: for now let's limit ourselves to some basic terms. A canoe paddle has a *blade* connected to a *T-grip* with a *shaft*. When we take a stroke, we *catch*, or *plant*, the paddle in the water and pull the boat forward in the *propulsion*, or *power*, phase. After this, when we remove the paddle from the water (or slice it through the water) to return it to the catch position for another stroke, comes the *recovery* phase. The side of the paddle blade that pulls against the water is called the *power face*, and the other side, the *back face*, or *nonpower face*. In a *dynamic* stroke the paddler pulls on the blade, whereas in a *static* stroke the paddler plants the blade and holds it, letting the momentum of the moving boat or the pull of the current complete the operation of the stroke.

And we need to define a few terms about the boat here. First is *trim*, or the balance of the boat from side to side and front to back. In general we want a neutral trim; that is, the weight should be distributed equally in both directions (many whitewater paddlers, however, prefer a slightly bow-light trim). The second is the related and critical concept of the *pivot point*. The ACA defines this as "the balance point of the craft around which the boat is trim—both fore-and-aft and side-to-side." Why is this important to the paddler? *Because it is around this point that the boat will*

At rest in calm water, a neutrally trimmed boat sits with the ends at equal depths in the water. The pivot point and center of gravity are both over the part of the hull deepest in the water. When under power, however, the hull dips forward into the trough of the wave that the bow pushes up. This causes the pivot point to move forward of the center of gravity.

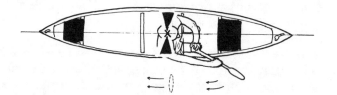

The relationship of the pivot point and the power stroke. Moving the blade farther from the pivot point creates a longer lever and more powerful stroke.

turn. The pivot point, by definition, sits most deeply in the water and therefore causes the most resistance to a turn. It is usually somewhere near the center (and centerline) of the boat. Although ease of turning depends on a number of design features, the place where the boat turns depends mostly on the location of the pivot point.

The pivot point is a dynamic concept. The first dynamic factor affecting the location of the pivot point is weight distribution. This is important when you consider it along with the Second Fundamental and with the general proposition that weight shifts are as important as paddle strokes. By shifting the weight in the boat, you alter the trim, and therefore the pivot point. The second dynamic force is the accumulation of external forces (which we'll look at in detail later) on the boat in the water.

Some simple examples: when the boat initially accelerates, the bow rises slightly, shifting the trim—and the pivot point—sternward. When the boat is moving forward under constant power, however, the bow tends to sink slightly in the wave it forms, moving the pivot point toward the bow. When the paddler shifts his weight to one side of the boat, as in an eddy turn, the pivot point shifts the same way.

Now imagine a line drawn through the pivot point of the boat from bow to stern. This line is a lever with which to turn the boat. A corrective stroke near the pivot point—where the lever is short—will have little effect. Take one near the ends (or beyond) and the boat will turn much more quickly. Upon this basic principle we will build our strokes. We'll cover both solo and tandem strokes, but we'll start with solo paddling and concentrate on each stroke in its pure form. Tandem strokes are, after all, mostly a combination of solo strokes.

One final word about conventions: all stroke descriptions are written for a right-side paddler unless otherwise noted.

Going Forward

The standard canoe power stroke is the forward stroke. It seems so simple, especially when executed by an expert. Just put the blade in the water and pull, right? Wrong. Canoes aren't built to go straight. Someone put the power interface (the paddle) off to one side of the boat, so the boat tries to turn every time you take a stroke. A single blade gives an unbalanced power delivery and requires that the paddler both steer and propel the boat with the same blade. Every canoe stroke is a compromise between power and correction, and the fact is that it is easier to get a canoe to turn than to go straight. This presents a problem on moving water for any canoe. Solo canoes, especially, often have problems building up enough momentum to punch through eddylines and cross contrary currents.

Developing an effective forward stroke, then, lies at the heart of canoeing. On flatter water, an effective stroke allows you to keep the power flowing for a longer period without tiring. The secret to effective paddle power is using the heavier muscles of the torso rather than the arms alone. Now let's see how it's done.

Imagine kneeling erect in the canoe with paddle in hand. Your left hand holds the T-grip of the paddle, fingers over the top, thumb underneath. The right hand slides down the paddle about three-quarters of the way down the shaft.

Now reach with the paddle as far forward as you can without bending. Pull back with your arms. That's the forward stroke most people do. Now thrust your right shoulder forward by rotating your body at the waist. Keep your bottom (right) arm straight, and move your top (left) hand out so that it's over the gunnel. Place the paddle in the water and, keeping your arms straight, pull your shoulder back instead of pulling with your arms, rotating your shoulders around as you do so. Use your waist—not your hips—as a pivot. That is the basic forward stroke. As you can see, most of the work is done by the torso. If you are not in good shape, or if you're not flexible, doing a good forward stroke may take some practice. But it's worthwhile, because almost all other strokes flow from this simple start. Let's review what we've learned and refine it a bit.

• Wind up the upper body by rotating your on-side shoulder forward, twisting your body at the waist (not the hips). Do not extend the paddle by leaning forward! Some 75 percent of the power of a forward stroke is delivered in the first five to seven inches of the paddle's travel, as the torso unwinds. It makes sense, then, to explode on a stroke; that is, to put everything you have into the first part of a forward stroke, rather than keeping the pull even. A corollary is that several short, powerful strokes (and a higher stroke rate) are better than one long one.

• Keep your right arm straight but not stiff. It is extended for the catch but bends back slightly during the power phase. The left arm stays slightly bent at about eye level.

• Keep the paddle vertical. At the start of the stroke, both hands should be across the gunnel, over the water, *with the T-grip out of the boat.* The top hand is held high and toward the on side. Dropping the top hand moves the blade away from the boat and away

The forward stroke: here the paddler has "wound up" his body by rotating at the waist and thrusting his right shoulder forward. He holds the paddle vertically out over the gunnel.

HOW LONG A PADDLE?

Beware of misinformation about the correct length canoe paddle. Some canoeing publications would have you choose a paddle that comes up to your chin when standing. In most cases this is far too long. Nantahala instructor Ed Daugherty recommends that when the blade is completely submerged, the T-grip should be at chin or eye level. That's when you're in the boat on the water. To find the right paddle-shaft length on dry land, sit or kneel on a bench or stair landing high enough to keep the paddle from touching the ground (simulating deep water), at about the same height that you sit or kneel in a boat. Now hold the paddle in front of you. When the *throat* of the blade (that is, the top of the tapered portion of the blade) is level with the top of the bench (and thus your knees), you should be looking at or slightly over the T-grip. This is approximately the correct shaft length, although you may vary it a few inches either way to accommodate your individual style. To that you must add the length of the blade. For most people a reasonable paddle dimension will be a shaft length of 56 to 59 inches with a blade 7½ to 8 inches wide and 18 to 20 inches long. I use a 60-inch canoe paddle, but I am six-foot seven . . .

MOCCIA ON THE FORWARD STROKE

- The bow paddler in a tandem boat should make sure that he pulls *straight back* (parallel to the boat's centerline) when doing a forward stroke. Sometimes it's tempting to follow the curve of the boat's hull on the forward stroke. This puts part of the stroke's power into a sweep stroke and forces the bow toward the paddler's off side.

- Keep the blade perpendicular to the boat's centerline: a twisted blade will spill water.

- If you see a splash, the blade isn't deep enough in the water when you start to pull back. The remedy is to drive the top hand down at the beginning of a stroke.

- To get maximum oomph, thrust the opposite (off-side) knee forward to where the paddle blade is planted.

- Are you rotating to the maximum? Draw a line through your shoulders (lay your paddle shaft on your shoulder blades for reference) and rotate your body until that line points to where you want the blade to enter the water.

- Relax. You don't need a death grip on the paddle.

—*Dave Moccia*

The forward stroke: the paddler here has delivered most of the power to the boat. The paddle shaft is still almost vertical, with both the paddler's hands over the gunnels. His torso has rotated back to its starting position, and the paddle shaft is at about the level of the paddler's knees. Bringing the paddle back any farther than this (unless for a correction stroke) wastes time and power.

from the centerline. Keep the power flowing parallel to the boat's centerline, and the closer and more parallel the stroke stays to the centerline, the less the boat will turn when power is applied. On really narrow boats you can sometimes move the blade *under* the boat.

- The paddle also stays more or less vertical as seen from the side. The paddler thrusts the blade forward slightly for the catch, then pulls the paddle back to vertical *and keeps it that way*. The stroke should make the transition from power to recovery as the blade passes the paddler's knees. Long strokes are unnecessary: they waste both time and power. The paddle transfers maximum power into the forward movement of the boat when it is perpendicular to the surface of the water. As the paddle deviates from the vertical position in a stroke, more and more power goes into pushing down on the water (pushing the boat up) or pulling up on the water (pulling the boat down).

What's the best way to learn the forward stroke? By watching someone who does it well, then practicing.

Now we have a good forward stroke. But there's still the problem of unbalanced power delivery. Apply power to the left and the canoe turns to the right, and vice versa. To keep the boat going in a straight line, the paddler must apply some kind of correction. Corrections, unfortunately, steal valuable time and power. Solo paddlers have to put in a corrective stroke with almost every power stroke. Tandem canoes fare better, since the bow and stern paddlers balance each other to some extent; but even so, the stern paddler must frequently make corrective strokes. Your goal, however, should be to move forward with minimal correction. Ultimately, you can reduce the number of corrections by using some river features to correct or by anticipating the effect each set of strokes will have.

There are two basic kinds of corrective strokes: the J-stroke and the stern pry. Although they are done differently, their effect is similar. Both strokes start with the forward stroke; the difference is that the J-stroke uses the power face of the paddle to apply the correction, but the stern pry uses the nonpower face. The J-stroke is quicker and works better when the boat is moving, but the stern pry is stronger and therefore more suitable for turns and abrupt changes in angle. In practice, however, they can be used virtually interchangeably.

The J-stroke allows a quick and subtle correction at

Keeping Straight

The J-stroke: the paddle has now come back behind the paddler's body, with the throat of the paddle resting on the gunnel. The thumb of the paddler's T-grip hand points down, and the paddle's power face points outward. Pulling inward on the T-grip applies the correction and completes the stroke.

the end of a stroke. That is why it is more effective when the boat is moving. Instead of going into a recovery as the paddle passes his knees, the paddler applies a correction by rotating the T-grip hand away from his body so that his thumb points *down*. The paddle turns in his shaft hand so that the power face of the paddle rotates outward, away from the canoe. Thus the power at the end of the stroke, instead of being applied parallel to the canoe's centerline, goes away from it at about a 45-degree angle. From overhead it looks like a capital letter *J*. The recovery from the J-stroke is slightly farther back than it is for the forward stroke, but should be no farther back than the centerline of the paddler's body. "But," you may say, "this is right next to the pivot point and, therefore, less effective than making the J farther back." True, but a quicker J saves time and allows the next forward stroke to begin with a minimum of delay. A small correction on each stroke equals one large correction. As your skill increases, you'll find this easier, and the boat will move forward much faster. A quick way to add more corrective power to the J is to move the shaft of the paddle inward and rest it against the gunnel. The added leverage increases the corrective power of the stroke. This variation of the J-stroke, called the on-gunnel or modern J-stroke, is recommended by the ACA.

TIP: *Allow the paddle shaft to rotate in your hand. Do not grip and rotate with your shaft hand. Let the T-grip do the work. This allows the shaft arm to relax and the right elbow to drop down toward the hip.*
                                              —Ed Daugherty

The stern pry is similar, and though it is a more powerful corrective stroke, it is less efficient, at least in terms of maintaining the forward power, than is the J. A *pry* is any stroke (except the on-gunnel J) that uses the gunnel for leverage. The stern pry differs from the J in two ways: it uses the nonpower face of the paddle, and the paddler does it farther back, giving it more corrective power. He slides the paddle back along the gunnel, slightly behind him, at the end of a forward stroke, turning the T-grip hand so that the thumb is

The stern pry correction: the paddle rests on the gunnel with the power face inward, and the paddler's thumb points up. Note that both the paddler's hands are still over the gunnel.

pointed *up*, then drops his top hand slightly so that the paddle blade angles toward the end of the canoe. His lower hand then holds the shaft against the gunnel, and with a quick pull on the T-grip he completes the stroke.

Obviously, this stroke results in a much longer recovery phase. Even so, the stern pry can be done very quickly and efficiently with practice.

TIP: When doing a stern pry, keep your pull short—four to six inches maximum. If the T-grip gets in front of your body, you've come in much too far.
                                        —Ed Daugherty

Now let's put it together and paddle forward. Forward, correct, forward, correct. The boat begins to pick up speed, gliding across the water. Forward, correct. For—wait! The boat's starting to swing sideways now, and its momentum begins to work against you. Correct! Correct! But it's too late. The boat lazily cir-

A BETTER SIDE TO PADDLE ON

Paddling on one side all day can be very tiring. Paddling on one side season after season can eventually injure your spine.

Switching sides will prevent this and is more efficient. Consider:

If you paddle on a lake on your left side using only forward strokes with no corrections, what happens? You turn right. To steer a straight course, you must do a corrective stroke to compensate.

Now you are on a river, which bends to the right. The fast water is on the outside of the bend (river left). If all you do is sit there, eventually water will pile up against your stern and the current will turn your boat clockwise (to the right). Suppose you're paddling around this bend on your left. To keep your boat straight, you have to correct not only for what your stroke does to the boat, but also for what the current does. This double correcting takes a lot of pry and can make you lose all your forward momentum and speed.

The solution is easy. Switch paddle on the side nearest the inside of the bend (the right side). If you do this with the right amount of power, the force of your forward stroke will match that of the current. No corrections needed.

For stern and solo paddlers it is usually more efficient to paddle on the inside of the bend.

                                        —*Dave Moccia*

ALTERNATIVES: SIT'N'SWITCH
When paddling long, skinny racing and touring boats in flat
water, there is another technique
for keeping the boat going
straight: variously called
sit'n'switch, the Minnesota
Switch, or somewhat grandilo-
quently, the North American
Touring Technique. Developed by
flatwater racers, this technique
has gained acceptance by cruisers
and whitewater paddlers as
well. It consists of using forward
strokes taken alternatively on
either side of the boat, using
them to balance the boat's tendency to turn. The solo paddler
takes several strokes on one side
of the boat, then switches hands
and puts in several more on
the other side, keeping the boat
straight under power. In theory,
any time lost by switching sides is
more than made up for by not
having to use the less-efficient
corrective strokes. It is usually
done with a bent-shaft paddle
while sitting rather than kneeling,
hence the name sit'n'switch.

Tandem boats use a similar system. Even if the paddlers are
stroking on opposite sides, the
canoe drifts slightly to one side.
By switching sides at the same
time, they can correct for this by
letting the canoe drift back the
other way. This switch is commonly used by marathon racers,
who are loath to waste time and
power on corrective strokes.
When switching sides, the bow
paddler, who can't see behind
him, sets the pace for the switch.

*Sit'n'switch paddlers use bent-shaft paddles and alter-
nate strokes on either side to keep the boat going straight.
This technique requires a long, straight hull to be effective. Note this hull's radical tumble home.*

cles, finally coming to rest as all your efforts go into
corrective rather than power strokes. What happened?
Your canoe built up momentum, which seems to give
it a mind of its own, even in flat water. In a sense it
does, because when the boat starts to turn, it keeps on
turning. Once this begins, corrective strokes become
progressively more difficult as the boat continues to
turn. The solution is practice. Learn to anticipate
when the boat is *starting* to turn, and apply the correction then. Once the turn becomes obvious, it's
really too late. A little correction on each stroke keeps
this from happening. Forward paddling is a balance
between power strokes turning the boat to the off side,
and corrective strokes turning the boat to the on side.

Now that we're paddling forward, let's think about turning. The simplest and most obvious turning stroke is the *sweep* stroke. In a sweep stroke, the paddler applies power in an arc around the pivot point, causing the boat to turn. Here we want the paddle to be as far away from the pivot point as possible in order to increase the leverage of the stroke. There are two basic variations of the sweep stroke: the *forward* sweep and the *reverse* sweep.

The forward sweep is executed as follows: put the paddle in the water beside the bow of the boat. Make sure the blade is all the way in the water. The blade should be vertical with the power face away from the boat. The thumb of the top hand points up. For maximum efficiency the shaft of the paddle should start out as parallel as possible to the centerline of the boat. Then plant the blade and rotate your torso, spinning the boat in a circle with your knee at the pivot point. Keep your arms straight and the paddle blade well away from the boat. The grip hand stays near the body (somewhere between navel and chest level), and it's usually helpful to choke up somewhat with the shaft hand. Finish by ending up with the shaft again parallel to the boat's centerline, this time with the paddle behind you. Pushing out with the T-grip hand during the last quarter of the stroke will add extra power. It's permissible to lean slightly forward or back, but remember to keep good posture during the stroke.

TIP: Body rotation is essential on the sweep stroke. A good way to ensure that your torso turns is to watch the blade and follow it all the way through the stroke; your torso will naturally rotate (for comparison, try a sweep while keeping your eyes and head straight ahead).

The reverse sweep is done basically the same way, except that the paddle blade starts at the stern of the boat and ends up at the bow. But it's hard to do a really effective reverse sweep all the way to the bow using the nonpower face of the paddle, so flip the blade over halfway through and complete the bow portion of the stroke using the power face. Think of it this way: start

Turning

The forward sweep: To start the stroke, the paddler rotates his shoulder forward and places the blade in the water as nearly parallel as possible to the hull.

With the paddle fixed in the water, he then spins the boat around, rotating his body as he does so. Looking at the blade encourages body rotation.

The sweep concludes with a stern draw, pulling the blade in towards the boat with the shaft hand. Note that during the entire stroke, both hands remained out over the water. The paddler continues to look at the blade and rotate his body.

a reverse sweep with the paddle near the stern, blade all the way in the water, shaft parallel to the centerline of the boat. The top hand has the thumb pointing up, and the nonpower face of the paddle is pointing away from the boat. The paddler's torso is turned—wound up—to the right. The paddler applies power and the boat begins to turn. When the paddle is at a right angle to the boat, the paddler flips the blade over so that his thumb is pointed down. He is now pulling against the power face of the blade, pulling the canoe alongside it. This is sometimes called the *compound reverse sweep.*

TIP: There are three common mistakes in making the sweep stroke: first, not getting the blade all the way in the water; second, not keeping the blade (as opposed to the shaft) vertical; and third, not keeping the paddle as far away from the pivot point of the boat as possible by extending the arms.

It's impossible to overemphasize the importance of building up speed and momentum in canoeing, especially for whitewater paddling. So avoid the common mistake of confusing the back stroke with the reverse sweep. The half reverse sweep (that is, from the stern to the point at a right angle to the boat) is a common corrective stroke on white water: it turns the boat back toward the paddler's on side after power strokes have made it veer to the off side. Done properly, it is a powerful corrective maneuver. Unfortunately, instead of doing a proper reverse sweep by sweeping the paddle out away from the boat, many paddlers simply put the paddle behind them and push forward, doing a back stroke. In one way the net effect is the same—the boat turns back to the on side. But the back stroke kills speed. In this sense it is a *negative* stroke, and you should avoid it. A reverse sweep, in contrast, reduces the boat's momentum much less.

Paddlers often experience extremes of frustration because they confuse the two strokes. You will see a paddler take a few powerful forward strokes to break through an eddyline. Then, when the bow swings away, he puts in an equally powerful back stroke, which totally stalls the boat. The lesson: learn at the

PRACTICE EXERCISE
Start with learning the strokes on flat water, so that you concentrate only on moving the boat without the additional complication of moving water or wind. Pick a distant point on the opposite shore and paddle toward it. When you get there, turn the boat using a turning stroke and start back again. Each time try to pick up your pace, going faster until you are crossing the lake as fast as you can paddle *under control.*

beginning to power the boat using *positive, forward strokes*, correcting as needed, rather than with reverse sweeps or, worse, back strokes. When the boat is accelerating from a virtual standstill, a stern pry usually works best as a correction.

Tandem Canoes

Tandem canoes have a somewhat easier time of going forward. Having a paddle blade on each side helps balance the power delivery, keeping the boat moving in a more or less straight line. Sitting farther away from the pivot point makes turning strokes like sweeps and draws more effective. Tandem paddlers also have the luxury of splitting the power and steering functions, usually by having the stern paddler steer (like any boat, a canoe steers better from the stern) and the bow paddler provide the power.

Despite these advantages, tandem canoeing is often more difficult and frustrating than solo canoeing. Why? One reason has more to do with psychology than with physics: it is almost irresistible to assign the blame for mistakes to one's canoeing partner. Many couples have switched from tandem to solo boats out of a desire for domestic tranquility. Another reason is coordination. Although tandem paddle strokes may be easier, weight shifts and balance are not. Tandem canoes move not by confrontation but by cooperation—often an elusive goal. The novice paddler finds it hard enough to predict what his own body will do on moving water, much less someone else's.

The forward stroke in a tandem canoe is virtually identical to the solo forward stroke. The bow paddler uses a pure forward stroke, and the stern paddler usually steers and provides corrective strokes (either J-strokes or stern pries) to keep the boat straight. It's easy for tandem paddlers to fall into the trap of trying to steer independently, both switching frantically from one side to the other. Unless this is part of a plan, it's usually best to paddle on one side and stick with it.

Although the stern paddler usually steers the tandem canoe, there are exceptions. For instance, when the canoe enters or exits an eddy, the bow paddler provides the lever for swinging the boat around. The other major exception is when the bow paddler leads the stern paddler to avoid an approaching hazard or obstacle. The bow paddler may not be as effective in turning the boat as the stern paddler, but he can see much better perched up front. The bowman *could* stop paddling, turn around, and say, "Hey, uh, Bob, there's a r—" *bam!* Far better for the sternman to read the bowman's body language and act accordingly. Each bow stroke has a complementary stern stroke, depending on what the paddlers want to accomplish.

Let's say that the bowman sees a rock dead ahead. He spots a clear chute to the right and decides to take it. Without saying a word, he (a lefty) puts in a forward sweep (or a cross bow draw, which we'll discuss later) near the bow, and the boat slowly begins to turn right. The sternman, seeing this, realizes that something is afoot and that they'd better turn the boat. He complements his partner's action by putting in his own stroke to turn right—a reverse sweep on the right. As long as the bowman continues sweeping (usually not more than a few strokes), the sternman follows, as in a dance. Now the bowman, heading for the chute, switches to a forward stroke. The sternman does likewise. When the boat is above the chute, the bowman draws the bow back to the left, straightening the boat, and the sternman follows with either a forward sweep or a stern draw. This system works well, provided the bowman's water-reading skills are up to the task.

You now have the basics to make the canoe go forward and to turn it. You *could* stop here and still have a lot of fun canoeing. But don't. There is more to learn— and more fun to be had.

FOUR

More Strokes

STROKES, STROKES, STROKES. Yes, there are differences. Between the cross turning high brace and the cross duffek. Between the cross back and the farback. And what about between the cross farback and the far-out? Many paddling books read like treatises on medieval theology, and the finer points of stroking are often argued with surprising passion. You will also run into purists, whatever they are, who will sneer at your efforts from behind mirrorshades. The question, especially at this point in the learning process, is not what's best, but what works for you. By this I don't mean learning just enough to get by, but expanding your paddling horizons in a reasonable, sensible manner. Start at the beginning, concentrating on perfecting a few basic strokes. But don't stay there. As your repertoire grows, look for efficiency and variety. Even more important, look to meld three elements—the boat, the water, and you—into a coherent whole. The basics outlined in the last chapter will, if you really master them, occupy you for a good while. But now it's time to move on. What follows is not a laundry list of canoe strokes (look elsewhere for that) but a logical progression of skills. Master the skills of this chapter and the next, and you'll be able to do almost anything you need to do on the river.

First let's expand our knowledge of corrective strokes. We have already mentioned the pry stroke briefly as an adjunct correction for the forward stroke. To pry, you place the paddle shaft on the boat's gunnel, submerge the blade, and pull inward on the T-grip. The pry uses the nonpower face of the paddle to push the canoe away from the paddler's on side. The recovery consists of *feathering* the blade (that is, turning the blade's edge toward the canoe) and returning the shaft to the upright position. This very powerful stroke—the leverage it generates is capable of tipping the boat over, especially on moving water—can also be used alone. The directional effect of the pry depends mostly on how far from the pivot point you place it. Done directly amidships, it moves the whole boat sideways. Placed away from the pivot point, it spins the boat, the more effectively as the distance increases.

The reverse of the pry stroke is the *draw* stroke. Whereas the pry pushes out, the draw pulls the boat toward the paddle. To execute the draw, the paddler

Prys and Draws

The stern pry begins with the paddle next to the boat with the power face outward. The paddler's body is rotated to the right, with both hands out over the water.

*Using the gunnel as a ful-
crum, the paddler pulls his
top arm in, pushing the
stern of the canoe away from
the paddle blade.*

first rotates his body so that he faces at a right angle
to the centerline of the canoe. Then he reaches both
hands out over the gunnel and plants the paddle,
keeping the blade as vertical as possible, and pulls the
boat toward the paddle.

That's the power phase. To recover, as the shaft
nears the gunnel, the paddler either feathers the blade
before lifting it from the water or slices it out of the
water by dropping his hand forward. As with the draw,
the directional effect varies in direct proportion to the

*The draw stroke has many
uses. Here the paddler
draws directly to the side of
the boat, planting the
paddle blade in the water
and pulling the boat toward
the blade.*

For a bow draw, the paddler drops his T-grip hand down onto his biceps, thus angling the blade towards the bow. His body rotation will now move the bow toward the paddle blade, spinning the boat.

stroke's distance from the pivot point. A draw made directly at the pivot point pulls the boat sideways, whereas a draw made nearer one end of the boat pulls that end around. When describing the draw stroke, paddlers often name the part of the boat toward which they pull: the bow draw or stern draw.

Draw strokes can be very effective turning strokes for both solo and tandem boats. A tandem boat, with

The stern draw: the stroke begins when the paddler places the blade in the water behind the boat, power face toward the hull, and pulls in with his bottom hand. Note body rotation and hands over the water.

STERN DRAW VS.
FORWARD SWEEP
Paddlers often confuse the stern draw with the forward sweep, both in concept and in execution. True, a forward sweep started amidships *does* look a lot like a stern draw. But look at each stroke's function:

• The forward sweep is a modified forward stroke that *pushes the bow* to the opposite side, around the pivot point. The top hand stays near to the gunnel and the paddler's body. The paddle shaft travels in an arc from the paddler's body.

• The stern draw *pulls the stern* directly to one side or the other. The canoe's stern moves in a straight line toward the blade.

So what's the difference? The result's the same. "Besides," you say, "I thought we weren't going to split hairs about strokes in this book."

Okay, but there really *is* a difference. Almost any boat steers more easily from the stern, and nowhere is this more true than in white water. Much of the time, the bow is buried in a wave or in the current, making corrective strokes far more effective at the stern. The stern draw, which pulls the stern around, works much better than trying to push the buried bow.

both paddlers sitting away from the pivot point and drawing on opposite sides, spins pretty fast. A solo paddler, on the other hand, sits at or near the pivot point. To turn, he must reach forward or sternward for an effective draw. Thus, the *bow draw* and the *stern draw* are mirror images of each other. As seen from the side, the paddle will be angled about 45 degrees from the vertical, but the blade remains vertical as seen from the bow or stern. In a bow draw the thumb points downward, and in a stern draw it points upward. The stern draw is a very important, effective, and underutilized stroke (for a more complete discussion of the bow draw, read on). The key elements of the stern draw follow:

• The paddler's body is rotated at a right angle to the centerline of the canoe. (Hands stay in the box, remember?) Experienced paddlers begin the stroke with their bodies rotated slightly less and then use the remaining torso rotation to add to the power of the stroke.

• The top hand stays approximately even with the paddler's face. The lower hand slides the blade slightly sternward of the paddler's body.

• Both hands are out past the gunnel and stay *over the water.*

• The left arm is kept straight, thumb pointing up. The right arm, aided by body rotation, pulls the boat toward the paddle, using the power face.

Tandem paddlers can also benefit from using the stern draw, particularly in white water where the stern paddler is often responsible for steering while the bow paddler provides power. Though the sternman can turn the boat pretty effectively toward his on side with a reverse sweep or a pry, turning the boat to his off side is more difficult: a forward sweep executed from the stern is not enough. A stern draw done behind the paddler as in a solo canoe, on the other hand, works very well.

Static Strokes

Until now all our strokes have been dynamic strokes; that is, the paddler has been pulling on the blade. In a static stroke, however, the paddler keeps the blade stationary. The *duffek* stroke, called the *post* by flatwater paddlers, is a good example of a static stroke. Here the paddler turns the boat by planting the paddle in the water near the bow and letting either the momentum of the boat or the current pull the boat around the paddle. An oft-used analogy is that of running down the street and grabbing a lamppost, using it to swing your body around. The key to the duffek-post is blade angle. Simply putting the paddle in the water for a draw, with the blade parallel to the centerline of the boat, will not turn the boat if the paddler merely holds the paddle still. Let's go back to the draw-stroke position for a moment: the paddler's body is rotated toward the draw, with the blade vertical and both hands over the water. The thumb of the top hand points sternward, parallel to the centerline of the boat. For the duffek, the paddler moves his left hand sternward while keeping his lower hand in place. He will end with his thumb pointing almost at his right bicep. This moves the blade toward the bow and away from the pivot point, increasing its effectiveness. Then he rotates the top hand so that his thumb points inward toward the boat. As a result, the blade begins to turn outward in the water, which pushes against the power face of the paddle, causing the boat to turn. The paddler can get more power by rotating his body so that the paddle moves away from the boat (thereby increasing the angle and resistance of the blade), and by rotating his top hand, again to increase the blade angle.

The setup for the onside duffek is virtually identical to that for the bow draw. The difference is that the duffek is a static stroke and the bow draw is a dynamic one. All it takes to convert a duffek to a bow draw is a good, hard pull.

Cross Strokes

Switching paddling sides can be the result of a deliberate policy, as with the sit'n'switchers, or the result of panic, as many novice whitewater paddlers know. True ambidexterity in paddling is like the Holy Grail: many will seek it, but few will attain it. For the whitewater paddler, switching paddling hands is clumsy and time consuming, and more important, it pulls the paddle out of the water. A split second here often makes the difference between capsizing and staying afloat. Yet sometimes an off-side stroke just has to be made. To resolve this dilemma, the *cross* stroke was born.

The cross stroke is a generic name for any stroke

taken on the paddler's off side *without* switching hands. These strokes are less powerful but much faster and surer. Although it sounds easy, any cross stroke requires a fair amount of body flexibility. The paddler takes his paddle out of the water on his on side, swings it across the boat, then puts it back in the water on the other side. This presents no problem for the top hand, but the bottom arm is now stretched across the paddler's body. The wider the boat, the more body rotation is required to get the blade vertical. Narrower boats definitely make this stroke easier, which is why you see it done more often in decked boats. However, cross strokes also work well when done in the relatively slender bow of a tandem boat. We also see now why it's a less powerful stroke than one done by switching hands: only a limited amount of body rotation is left for power.

Cross strokes, like draws, are classified according to their function. The most important ones are the *cross forward*, the *cross draw*, and the *cross duffek*. Cross strokes require practice, and some prior stretching exercises aren't a bad idea, either.

The cross forward stroke is an off-side clone of the on-side forward stroke. It's also one of the few strokes in which it's okay to lean forward. Swing the paddle across the boat and plant the blade in the water as far forward as you can. The same considerations apply here as with the on-side forward stroke: keep the blade vertical throughout the stroke, and keep the stroke parallel to the boat's centerline. To recover, feather the

The cross forward stroke: the paddler reaches across the hull and executes a forward stroke without changing hands.

The cross forward stroke in action: Kent Ford recovers the blade by feathering it slightly and lifting it straight up. A cross forward stroke should not come back behind the paddler's knees.

blade (forward, with the thumb up), lift it out of the water, and plant it again.

The cross draw and the cross duffek are the off-side equivalents of the on-side draw and the duffek, and are used for the same purposes. Like the on-side strokes, the setup is virtually identical; the difference is that the paddler pulls on the draw, but lets the water do the work with a duffek. In both strokes the paddle is angled toward the bow at perhaps 45 degrees. The paddler's thumb on his top hand is pointed up, with the shaft hand straight across the body and the top hand cocked so that the T-grip is next to the paddler's shoulder. For the cross draw, the paddler rotates his body as far as possible toward his off side, plants the paddle so that the blade is perpendicular to the water, and pulls the boat toward the paddle. Unlike the cross forward stroke, the cross bow draw can generate considerable power through body rotation. Done correctly, it uses almost no arm motion. To recover, the paddler lifts the blade, rotates his body out again, and plants the paddle.

With the cross duffek, the paddler may choose to hold the blade slightly more vertical in the fore and aft

The cross draw: the paddler rotates his body so that the paddle crosses the hull, then plants the blade parallel to the hull with his thumb up. His body rotation pulls the boat towards the paddle blade, spinning the bow around.

plane. As with the on-side version, he is able to control the amount of resistance (and therefore power) by rotating the blade away from the canoe's centerline. The greater the blade's rotation, the more power is transmitted to the boat.

Balance and Weight Shifts

So far, in our discussion of strokes, we have assumed that the boat stays flat on the water. Now it's time to change that assumption. One of the hardest things for novice canoeists to learn is the necessity of leaning the boat. They associate boat lean, quite naturally, with tipping over. However, you'll have to learn to lean the canoe sooner or later, since virtually all varieties of paddling require that you use it, as do many modern boat designs (more on that later). On moving water it is a necessity: you must lean the boat to compensate for the overturning forces of the current. This is one of the many paradoxes of white water. You lean the boat to avoid flipping, even though it seems like you'll turn over when you do.

Current differentials in a river can upset a boat by torquing against the bottom. Forces of thirty to fifty foot-pounds trying to rotate the hull upstream are not uncommon. How do we compensate for this? In two ways: first, by leaning the *boat* away from the current (that is, downstream), and second, by shifting the paddler's weight to the downstream side of the boat. Differentiate between boat lean and the leaning paddler. To understand this, remember the Second Fundamental: keep your weight over the boat. To achieve this, you must lean the boat and not your body. Leaning the boat turns the rounded edges of the hull toward the current and gives the water less purchase than the relatively straight sides of the boat. The paddler shifts his weight by pushing down with one knee, directly compensating for the overturning force of the current. Along with weight shift, remember the First Fundamental: sit up straight in the boat.

Now let's see how *not* to do it. Our novice paddler pulls into the current from an eddy, knowing that a swim awaits him if he does not lean downstream. As the boat crosses the eddyline, he thrusts his body out over the boat's gunnel and puts his weight on the paddle. What's the problem here? He has violated two paddling fundamentals at once: by leaning his body instead of sitting straight, he cannot take effective strokes or make body moves, and since his weight is over the gunnel instead of over the boat, the hull sits flat on the water, prey to the upstream forces. The downstream gunnel will rise and hit his chest, and if

A good peel-out. Both paddlers have their weight shifted downstream on their right knees. Although the boat is leaned downstream, the paddlers are sitting relatively straight up with their weight still over the boat. Current goes L to R.

the force is sufficient, he will be pitched back on the upstream gunnel and capsize. In any case he won't be able to do anything effective until after the boat has matched the speed of the current.

The downstream lean is a nearly universal rule for canoeing, but sometimes there is some confusion as to just what "downstream" means. As we saw in chapter 1, water often flows upstream. Therefore, the rule might be better stated if we said that the correct lean is always in the direction of the current—into your turn.

Let's look an another example: the canoe is coming out of the main current into an eddy. The water in the main current flows downstream, but the eddy flows upstream. As the boat crosses the eddyline, the water suddenly changes direction. If the paddler's weight is over the centerline (which it normally would be with the boat moving downstream at the same speed as the water) or shifted downstream in relation to the main current, he won't be able to compensate when the boat suddenly encounters the opposite current. At the moment the boat begins to cross the eddyline, then, the paddler must progressively shift his weight toward the obstacle that created the eddy. As the boat completes the eddy turn and faces upstream in relation to the main current, the paddler's weight shifts back onto both knees. The easiest way to keep this straight in your mind is to compare it to riding a bicycle: always lean into the turn.

Waves present a similar problem. Since river waves

The eddy turn: here the boat breaks across the eddy line. The paddlers have shifted their weight so that the boat leans toward the obstacle that created the eddy (i.e., into the turn). The stern paddler executes a stern draw, while the bow paddler reaches out to plant a duffek into the eddy.

don't move, the river's current must flow over them. This means that water flows *up* the face of a wave. Gravity, on the other hand, tries to pull the boat back down the face of the wave, slowing the boat's progress. The counteraction of current and gravity has the same effect as crossing from one river current to another flowing in the opposite direction—it tends to flip a sideways-facing boat back upstream. As if that were not enough, the top of the wave sometimes breaks back upstream on the boat. The rule here is to lean toward the upstream face of a wave, especially one that's breaking, a little more than you think is necessary. When you get over the top, however, you must "uncompensate" or you'll flip. (For more on handling waves, see chapter 6.)

TIP: *When sideways in the river and paddling through big waves, paddle on the downstream side. It's easier to brace into an upcoming wave. When paddling in shallow, rocky water, however, paddle on the upstream side. It's better to let your paddle get pulled over the rocks than have it jerked out of your hands under the boat, which would probably turn you over.*

—Dave Moccia

Holes work in much the same way. The white cushion of a hole may stop the forward motion of a boat, especially when you drop into one sideways. If this

BALANCE EXERCISE: THE CONFIDENCE LEAN

"Trust me": it's an essential concept for tandem canoeing but sometimes a hard one to develop. Start with the confidence lean, in which tandem partners support each other. Find some flat water, stow your paddles, and sit astride the seats, each facing sideways in the opposite direction. Brace yourself in the boat (wrapping your legs around the seats works fine). Looking at each other, lean backward. Talk to each other about what's happening. Keep on leaning back until your bodies are over the water, then parallel with the surface. Keep on going until you get your head wet, and then—slowly—come back up. This works best for persons of similar size, but a heavier person can compensate for weight differences by sliding inward as the lighter person slides outward. Try it—it's a real confidence builder.

The confidence lean—a good way to develop faith in your partner.

happens, look out, because unless you quickly shift your weight downstream and lift the hull, you'll be *windowshaded*. That is, you get flipped upstream fast enough to turn the world into a foamy blur. Getting in and out of holes is a more advanced subject than this chapter permits, but the basics are the same. Keep your weight over the boat, lean the hull downstream—and try to paddle out one side of the hole or the other.

Leaning the boat also makes turns easier, because most boats, even svelte flatwater canoes, turn faster when they're leaned. Shifting your weight toward the paddle while executing a turning stroke brings it off more quickly and easily. Both whitewater paddlers and freestyle flatwater paddlers customarily lay the boat over to the gunnels to turn.

Braces

Canoeing braces are the third kind of canoe stroke—the stabilizing stroke. We have deliberately left them until now for two reasons: first, brace strokes can become a crutch that slows your paddling progress, and second, this is the type of stroke most likely to injure you.

THE LOW BRACE. The canoe low brace is a powerful stroke. It acts as an outrigger, forcefully pushing the back face of the paddle against the surface of the water, providing enough leverage to overcome all but the strongest capsizing forces. Unfortunately, it is available on only one side, which is why many canoeists instinctively favor their on side by shifting their weight slightly that way when paddling. Because the low brace can get them out of jams, some paddlers rely on it too much, almost to the exclusion of other

The low brace: note that both hands are in the water. The power face of the paddle faces down, and so does the paddler's head. To right the boat, he pulls up on his T-grip hand.

strokes. At the first sign of trouble, out goes the paddle, and the drift begins. You can float through a lot of water this way, but it's better to paddle under control, and to be in control on moving water, you need to be moving under power.

To do an effective low brace, get the paddle as flat on the surface of the water as possible. Both hands must be out over the water. The shaft of the paddle should be more or less perpendicular to the boat (and therefore in the box). Initially, both hands are straight, and the shaft hand stays that way to act as a fulcrum. The T-grip hand goes into the water first, then the paddler pulls up, forcing the paddle blade down and the boat up.

The low brace requires a somewhat different body motion than the strokes we've tried so far. It can hurt you. Shoulder dislocations are less common in canoes than in kayaks, but they still happen. Usually, they occur when the paddler lets his arm stray out of the box and the paddle blade bumps something. To reduce the danger, rotate your body to the side during the brace and keep your hands in the box. Do not put your hands behind you to brace while keeping your body facing forward. Remember the Fourth Fundamental: the body follows the blade. In this case, your head stays over your T-grip hand.

Two other body parts whose motion is significant are the head and the on-side knee. If the boat is equipped with thigh straps, the paddler can help right the boat during a low brace by pulling up with his on-side knee. This movement is important in bracing and mandatory in rolling an open canoe. The paddler's head, though it isn't actually in the water (at least, not yet), controls much of the motion of the rest of the body. The head motion is essential for controlling weight shifts. Generally speaking, when the head goes one way, the body goes the other. So when the head goes down, the body—and therefore the boat—comes up.

Try an exercise to demonstrate to yourself how the motion of the head controls that of the body. Kneel on a flat, comfortable surface like the rug in your living room. Push your head down to the right without leaning over. Notice how your body bows out to the *left*.

MOCCIA ON THE LOW BRACE

The low brace rights the boat when it tips to your paddling side. Timing and proper body motion are more beneficial than noise and splash. *Low brace: knuckles down.* Rotate both wrists forward, knuckles facing the water, paddle blade facing the water, shaft horizontal. Keep your head low (on the paddle shaft). Reach straight out to your side or a little in front of you. Face the paddle with both hands *outside* the gunnel. Your T-grip hand hits the water first. When it touches the water, your head should be directly above the T-grip. As soon as your T-grip hand hits the water, push down with your shaft hand, and at the same time pull up with your T-grip hand, just enough to clear the gunnel, then pull it in to the center of the boat. Keep your head low and over the T-grip hand. When the T-grip hand comes into the center of the boat, your head should come in also. Your body will follow your head, shifting your center of gravity back over the centerline.

Brace either at your side or in front of you, and face your paddle blade *at all times*. If you are in the wrong position, it's very easy to strain or dislocate your shoulder—even on a lake. I don't advise practicing low braces until you've developed a feel for the body and the paddle.

—Dave Moccia

Now reverse the direction of your head. Your body also reverses, bowing out in the opposite direction.

Let's look at how this works when you are paddling. Still in the same position, put your hands out toward your right side (lefties reverse the directions). Now lean over so that you're supporting yourself on your hands. Most probably your head is still upright, although your body is now leaning very far to the right. Now, with your head still upright, push yourself back up on your knees. If you're like most people, you probably gave your head a little push to the left as you came up. This is a common intuitive motion, *but it's not what you want to do*. Drop back onto your hands again. Look over your left shoulder. Notice how your body weight is shifted *to the right*, opposite your head. Move your arms slightly behind you now. When your head goes left and your arms get behind you (out of the box), you are in a prime position for a shoulder injury. Worse, your brace will be ineffective, since the shift of your body weight will tend to offset the power of your brace. Yet this is exactly the way many people brace.

Now try it the right way. Go back down with your hands on the floor. Make sure your hands are beside rather than behind you. Now rotate your body so that your head is facing your hands. With your head facing down like this, your body weight has shifted *away* from your on side. This is what you want—the weight shift now complements your brace, and a shoulder injury is far less likely.

THE HIGH BRACE. The term *high brace* has, in recent years, meant two entirely different strokes. Some paddlers have even maintained that there is really no such thing in canoeing.

What used to be called the high brace was similar to the low brace, except that it was done with the power face of the paddle against the water. This type of high brace is less effective than the low brace because it is more difficult to get the paddle blade flat on the surface of the water. This is especially true in an open canoe, where the paddler sits fairly high above the water. It does work well in a kayak, however, where the paddler sits much lower. Like the low brace, its purpose is to keep the boat from capsizing toward the paddler's on side.

The (new) high brace: used to stop the boat from tipping over on the paddler's off side.

What's now called the high brace, as illustrated in the ACA *Instruction Manual*, is similar in that it is still done on the paddler's on side with the power face of the paddle. However, its purpose has been changed. Now it's used for keeping the canoe from capsizing toward the canoe's *off* side. Instead of putting a brace *down* on the surface of the water, the paddler uses the high brace almost as a draw, keeping the angle of the paddle high and pulling against the water to overcome the boat's off-side torque.

There is no hook on the end of your paddle to pull the boat back down. What rights the boat is shifting your body weight over the high side. The more sudden the tip, the more quickly and violently you have to throw your upper body over. If you have good balance and are loose at the hips, you know how much weight to throw and when to bring it back. The rest of us keep from falling in the drink by landing and catching ourselves on a high brace.

For the high brace, knuckles point up. Here you are hanging under your paddle with both elbows slightly bent. To the uninformed it looks like a draw stroke done straight out from your hips, but the paddle shaft is more horizontal. Rotate your upper body slightly to your on side. Your T-grip hand is level with your forehead and in front of it. The shaft hand is extended but with a bend in the elbow. As with a low brace, the paddle goes at a right angle to the boat's centerline or a little forward.

Here's the sequence. Your boat tips to the off side.

BRACING PRACTICE

A good way to practice bracing on a lake is to have a friend first tip your boat to one side without letting go. This will take your mind off getting wet and let you concentrate on good technique. Next let him tip you and let go. Don't change hands with the paddle. Next it's your friend's turn to have some fun, by tipping you to either side without warning. Now switch paddle hands and start from the beginning.

To keep your friend healthy, don't let him line up with the path of the paddle. To keep yourself healthy, have the friend watch your arm and head position.

—*Dave Moccia*

You throw your upper body's weight over the high side and catch yourself on the high brace. To bring yourself back upright, shift your weight to your on-side knee and at the same time pull your paddle blade into the boat by driving your shaft elbow into your hip, and push out slightly on your T-grip. This will bring your paddle shaft to a more vertical position. Then pull your head into the center of the boat.

Nonessential Strokes

No discussion of stabilizing strokes would be complete without these. The *air brace* is just what the name implies: the paddle stays in the air, waiting for something to happen (it usually does). The time for the air brace is after you've run through the rapid, to announce your success. Otherwise, the best place for the paddle is in the water. Even a forward stroke provides a surprising amount of stability, so keep paddling. Momentum enhances control.

The *gunnel grab* is the last-ditch effort of many canoeists. Compared with the water rushing alongside, the gunnel seems to offer some security when balance fails. Wrong. Not only is it a fragile reed to grasp, it keeps you from doing a stabilizing stroke that might otherwise save the day. Pretend the gunnels are electrified, and keep your hands off!

The other nonstroke is the *paddle twirl*. Paddle twirling doesn't move the boat, but it really *looks*

The air brace: of somewhat limited utility unless you are able, as this paddler is doing, to rely on balance rather than a brace.

The paddle twirl.

good. And it's not all show. If you can twirl your paddle while doing some halfway-difficult maneuver, like surfing a wave, it shows you've mastered the move and have the skill and balance to do it. Probably the most important use of the paddle twirl, however, is to cover errors stylishly. Let's say you come down a rapid, do everything wrong, wobble through but somehow save yourself from flipping. As you stabilize, you remember your friends are watching. Instead of staring blankly in terror, you grin and twirl your paddle, hoping they'll think you did it all on purpose. If you're really cool, try it in that last moment when you know it's too late, just before you hit the water.

The paddle twirl is relatively simple to do. Hold your shaft hand straight above your head (okay, it's out of the box), palm flat with the paddle shaft resting on it. The balance point of the paddle (usually near the paddle's throat) goes on your palm. Now grasp the shaft and give it a spin, letting it rotate on your open palm. Pick an unobstructed area to try it, and practice.

Tandem Complementary Strokes

The solo canoeist has only himself to worry about. He uses paddle strokes in a relatively pure form, combining them as necessary, but doing only one at a time. Boaters in tandem canoes, on the other hand, have to cooperate. We've already mentioned how, although the stern paddler generally steers, he often follows the bow paddler's strokes because the bowman sees farther. Now it's time to look closer at that relationship, to see how tandem strokes fit together in pairs. This will be absolutely essential when we start with moving-water maneuvers in the next chapter.

Going forward requires little explanation. Both the bowman and sternman paddle forward. The sternman corrects when necessary. Turning strokes, however, require cooperation.

	LEFT TURN	RIGHT TURN
Bow-left	Bow draw	Cross bow draw *or* on-side forward
Stern-right	Stern draw *or* forward sweep	Pry *or* reverse sweep
Bow-right	Cross bow draw *or* on-side forward	Bow draw
Stern-left	Pry *or* reverse sweep	Stern draw *or* forward sweep

The pairings should be obvious by now. A cross draw by a right-handed paddler should be an immediate signal to a lefty sternman to put in a pry or reverse sweep, and so on. This type of paddle signaling requires some practice, so start on a lake. It also requires the sternman to pay attention to what's going on in the bow. It seems a small exception to the Fifth Fundamental, on looking far ahead, but it isn't really, since it is now the bow paddler, who can see farther, who must take up the vision for the boat.

Moving Backward

Finally, there are back strokes. We have saved this subject until last because these are the strokes least used, as well as some of the most difficult to do well. Paddlers, especially novice–intermediates, seldom use reverse strokes because they are usually fully occupied with forward ones. Back strokes are often an unwanted complication at this stage, and you will be able to do anything you need to do without them. If you are starting out, you may safely skip this section. Later, however, you may find that proficiency with reverse strokes becomes part of the overall mastery of the boat.

The *back stroke*, or *reverse stroke*, is pretty much the converse of the forward stroke. The paddler rotates his body toward his on side, plants his blade at a point almost beside him, and unwinds his body, pushing the canoe backward. He holds his paddle in the normal position for a forward stroke and uses what in the normal forward stroke would be considered the back face of the paddle (here, if you want to get technical, it's really the power face). In tandem boats, moving the boat backward is straightforward, since with a neutrally trimmed boat the pivot point remains in the same place. The big difference is that it is now the bow paddler who steers. For the bow paddler, the corrective strokes of choice are the pry and the reverse sweep.

The solo paddler has a more difficult time of it because he is usually sitting slightly behind the pivot point and often has the boat trimmed slightly to the stern. This makes the boat even more likely to turn when going backward, not to mention that he has the same old problem with unbalanced power delivery. As with the solo forward stroke, a correction is necessary for almost every reverse power stroke. There are three primary solo back strokes (as well as some others if you care to look them up): the back stroke, the compound back stroke, and the cross back stroke. Let's look at each in turn.

The simple *back stroke* comes in two varieties: the simple back stroke, which we've already described, and the *farback stroke*. To implement the farback stroke, the paddler rotates his body as far toward his on side as he can, so that he is nearly facing the stern. He then reverses his paddle and plants the power face almost vertical *behind him*. The farback stroke goes only from this point to about the plane of the paddler's

The farback stroke: the paddler rotates his body and reaches behind him, pulling forward with the power face of the paddle. It is essentially a forward stroke turned around.

body. Then the paddler feathers the blade and begins another stroke. The advantage of the farback stroke is that it puts the stroke behind the paddler and in front of the pivot point, pulling the boat along and making it somewhat easier to keep the boat going straight in a reverse direction.

If you combine the simple back stroke with the farback, you have the *compound back stroke*. Instead of ending the stroke level with the paddler's body, the paddler flips the blade over and continues into a simple back stroke, ending with a small correctional pry. As the blade passes his body, the paddler must quickly reverse the orientation of the blade—starting with the power face, and then pushing against the nonpower face.

TIP: To remember the sequence of events in the compound back stroke, think pull, push, pry: pull the paddle to your hips, then push past your knees, then pry toward the bow, sliding your hand up at the end of the stroke.

The corresponding cross stroke is the *cross back stroke*. Though powerful, it requires the most body flexibility of any canoe stroke. For that reason alone, however, it's a good stroke to learn because it really forces you to use body rotation. To do a cross back, start with the paddle on your on side, beside your body. Now lift the paddle as if for a cross draw. Continue rotating your body past what you think is a reasonable point to stop. The plane of your shoulders should be parallel to the centerline of the boat, with your body facing your off side. Now plant the paddle directly beside you. Your right (on-side) arm should be drawn tightly across your chest. For this stroke, you will use the power face of the paddle, so you will need to rotate your wrists sternward until the blade is at a right angle to the centerline of the canoe. If you don't feel like you're tied in a knot by now, you're either exceptionally flexible or you're doing something wrong. Take the stroke by rotating even farther back (yes, I know) and unwinding your body enough to pull the boat backward.

Although the movement in the cross back stroke is

The cross back stroke: the paddler rotates his body so that the paddle crosses the boat, placing the paddle blade (power face toward the bow) as far back as possible. Forward rotation of the body moves the boat.

only a few inches, the resulting movement of the boat is much more. The cross back stroke is almost completely distilled torso motion, since it's nearly impossible to use your arms in that position. You can use the cross back alone or in combination with on-side back strokes.

We've covered a lot of paddling territory in the last two chapters. Starting with the forward stroke and the corrections that go with it, we've progressed through the turning and correction strokes—sweeps, prys and draws—to the stabilizing brace strokes and then to reverse strokes. Although we have not covered every possible stroke, these are enough to move a canoe through almost any water. Many of the other strokes are simply variations on these. The only major omission has been the open canoe roll (which is covered in chapter 7).

The other important theme has been weight shifts and distribution. You can have picture-perfect strokes, but unless you are able to put your weight in the right place at the right time, they will be for naught on moving water.

Having covered water and the mechanics of canoe driving, it's time to get out and do it. We close with a quote from the Ayatollah of Flat Water, Harry Roberts, who neatly sums it up:

"Technical instruction about paddling is not to be confused with paddling itself. Paddling is a way of thinking, a way of weaving yourself into the grand figure of wind, wave, water, earth, and canoe. Technical skill is that which frees you from fear, anxiety and fatigue, and that which lets you partake more fully of the totality that is paddling."

FIVE

Moving-Water Basics

AN OLD COWBOY was talking about his job. He said that you didn't really have to know very much to be a cowboy, you just had to know what a cow would do. Much the same thing can be said about canoeing on moving water: you just have to know what the water will do. But simple cerebral understanding is not enough. At some point both the knowledge and skill of paddling must enter into the instinctive level. Recalling Harry's injunction at the end of the last chapter, here is where we begin to weave ourselves into that grand figure of wave and water with our canoe.

We now enter into the third major area of paddling technique, after body movement and balance and the placement of the paddle in the water. It is the place of the boat on the river.

If you have dutifully mastered the strokes on flat water, you are ready to try the new, exciting, and at first seemingly random factor of moving water. I have deliberately avoided calling this chapter *Whitewater Basics*, because the techniques we'll learn here apply to *all* moving water.

The three elemental moves for placing a boat where you want it on moving water are the eddy turn, the peel-out, and the ferry. All moving-water techniques, no matter how advanced, are built on these three, plus a knowledge of the ways of moving water.

The *eddy turn* allows us to enter eddies. These are relatively calm stretches of river in which to stop for rest or scouting. It's much more convenient to stop in a midriver eddy than to pull over to shore. Eddies also allow you to break down sections of river, especially those with rapids, into more manageable chunks. Eddies, and not backpaddling, are the real brakes of canoeing. Paddlers can also use eddies for upstream travel. The *peel-out* gets us out of an eddy and back into the main current again, with the boat going downstream.

There may be times, however, when you don't want to continue downstream. Perhaps you need to cross the river above an obstacle. The *ferry* allows you to travel across the current without going downstream.

Put these three together and you can move, within the limitations imposed by the force of the current and your skill, almost anywhere on the river: upstream, downstream, back and forth, even stay in one spot. Unfortunately, many canoeists avoid eddy turns and peel-outs because they associate them with frigid swims. So let's see how to do each move.

Eddy Turns

Before starting the mechanics of eddy turns, let's quickly review what we're trying to do and what forces are involved. Consider a canoe approaching a downstream eddy in a three- to four-mile-per-hour current. If the canoeists are paddling forward (as they should be), they may add two to three miles per hour to this speed. The eddy is flowing upstream, probably a little slower than the downstream current, let us say at two miles per hour. Since the canoe is moving at the same speed as the current, there is no torque on the bottom of the canoe, and the paddlers have their weight more or less over the centerline of the boat. Now the canoe reaches the eddyline and starts across it. The current *differential* may now amount to nearly ten miles per hour. The bow of the boat, as it crosses the eddyline, suddenly is no longer moving at the same speed as the current. A torque, or turning force, is now abruptly applied to the *bow* and *bottom* of the canoe as the eddy tries to turn the bow of the canoe upstream. As more of the canoe enters the eddy, this force becomes

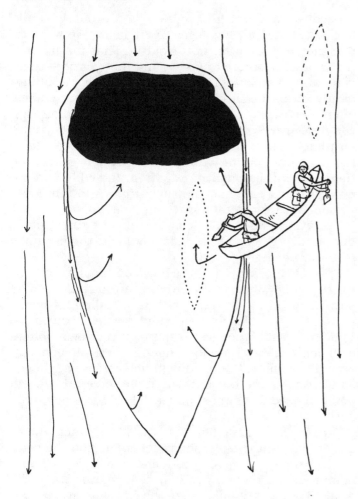

The correct angle for an eddy turn. The boat enters the eddy at a 45-degree angle to make use of the torque applied to it by the opposite-flowing main and eddy currents. This force turns the boat to face upstream, positioning it for a peel-out. A less aggressive angle of approach would not allow the boat to push through the rejector line— the swiftly flowing water squeezed between the eddy-line and the main current.

stronger, until finally the canoe leaves the main current altogether and enters the eddy, matching its speed. At this point, the torque disappears.

This torque acts in two ways. First, it turns the bow around to face upstream. That's fine, and just what we want to position us for a peel-out or ferry. But it also does something a lot more nefarious. It pulls on the underside of the boat and will pull it right out from under an unsuspecting or timid paddler. One minute you're upright, looking good, and the next you're trout scouting.

Ah! But if that's the problem, why not just slow down to enter an eddy? Or enter it farther down, where it's not so strong?

Because we *want* it to pull the bow around. Think (for just a second) like a hydro engineer. We want to *use* the river's power, not avoid it. That torque can turn your boat more quickly—and more easily—than you can. Another reason, which will become abundantly clear the first time you try it, is that eddies often aren't that easy to get into. The water along an eddyline speeds up even faster than the main current, forming a faint but very real *rejector line*. A slow-moving canoe, or one without enough angle going into the eddy, will be pushed away from the eddy and on downstream. This can be frustrating. And one final reason: once you get it figured out, it's *fun*.

Everything we've said so far about eddy turns, peel-outs, and ferries can be seen in relation to three simple factors: *speed, angle,* and *lean.*

Speed is the velocity of the boat coming into or leaving the eddy. When you're entering an eddy, the downstream current is working with you, adding its speed to yours. When leaving an eddy, however, you must build up most of the needed speed on your own—often a difficult task in a solo canoe. So get this concept straight—you must forcefully punch across eddylines. The stronger the current, the more force and speed you will need. It's almost impossible to have too much speed for this.

Angle refers to the bearing of the boat when entering or leaving the eddy. Too much angle and the boat slows before hitting the eddyline, too little (a more common problem) and you fail to penetrate the eddy at all. The boat should cross the eddyline at about a 45-degree angle. In reality, however, the angle of approach will be closer to 90 degrees because of the effect of the rejector line. That is, if you approach the eddy from a nearly 90-degree angle, after the rejector line does its work you will probably end up at a 45-degree angle.

TIP: *To tap the power of an eddy fully, hit it as high as possible, that is, as close to the obstacle that created it as you can. This is where the eddy is the strongest. Ideally, you should barely skim the rock that is creating the eddy and just barely avoid hitting it as the boat turns.*

Lean is really weight shift; it consists of leaning the boat, not your body. Which way do you lean? Think as if you were riding a bicycle around curves. You always lean the boat *into* the turn when entering or leaving an eddy by shifting your weight slightly and pushing down with the inside knee as you cross the eddyline. The greater the current differential, the more you must lean the boat to avoid flipping toward the outside.

Eddy turns require you to aim, in effect, at a moving target. That is, the target stays still while *you* move. This presents a nice problem that requires some practice to solve: hit the eddy too high and you risk clipping the rock that created it; hit it too low and you may miss it altogether. You must be close enough to the eddy to set the correct angle and drive into it as you pass. Novices usually start too far away from an eddy and don't leave themselves enough time to get over, thereby hitting the eddy too low or missing it altogether. Then they overcompensate by coming too close, which makes it impossible to set the entry angle correctly. Passing too close also does not allow the paddler to develop enough drive into the eddy, but instead tends to carry the boat past the eddy downstream. It is a problem best solved by experience.

Peel-outs

A peel-out is the reverse of an eddy turn. Having once attained the haven of an eddy, you can use a peel-out to get back into the main current. Peel-outs are easier than eddy turns in that the paddler is relatively stationary and does not have to aim while on the move, but they are harder (especially for solo canoes) in that they require the paddler to develop a considerable amount of momentum in a rather short distance. When you are coming into an eddy, the downstream current adds speed, but a boat needs this same amount of momentum to get back out of an eddy. When you are making a peel-out, however, although the *angle* and *lean* factors are more or less the same, you have to generate *speed* from a near standstill.

Although when peeling out you do not have to deal with the rejector line of an eddy (it's on the outside), it is possible for you to be shoved right back into an eddy that you're trying to leave. This is usually the novice paddler's biggest bugaboo. The tendency is to take a few forward strokes, until the bow of the boat reaches the eddyline, then drop to a brace. Deprived of its momentum, the boat coasts to a stop about halfway across the eddyline, spins around, and either rebounds back into the eddy or drifts lazily down the eddyline, frequently ending up where it started.

Let's quickly analyze why this happens. The paddler knows he must lean downstream or he will flip when entering the main current, so this is usually where his attention is focused. Since he is afraid to lean his boat, he gives it a few forward strokes and then leans his body across the downstream gunnel and goes into a low brace to support his body weight. Once he assumes this position, he surrenders control of his boat to the river.

The expert paddler begins paddling forward with a good, hard stroke toward the eddyline, then as the bow begins to cross it, he progressively shifts his weight to his downstream knee, tilting the edge of the boat up and away from the clutching fingers of the current. His weight remains centered over his downstream knee, and he continues to paddle forward until the boat has entirely cleared the eddyline. Then he puts in a turning stroke, if needed, to finish bringing the bow around downstream. If he has done the peel-out correctly, however, the water will have already done most of the turning for him. The paddler never braces or loses control of the boat to the current, and is whisked away downstream with a minimum of effort: he lets the river do much of the work. On the whole, it's better to develop boat lean, balance, and momentum than a killer low brace.

A word or two about vision may also be helpful here. As just mentioned, most novices concentrate their vision on the eddyline. This means that mentally (and quite often physically) the boat stops right there, since that's as far as your mind has processed the move. Remember what we said about visualization? Hold the picture of the complete move in your mind, and concentrate on where you want to go, rather than where the difficulty lies. Now apply this to an eddy turn. Look *into* the eddy where you want to go, not at the eddyline, where you *don't* want to stop. On a peel-out, look out into the main current where you want to end

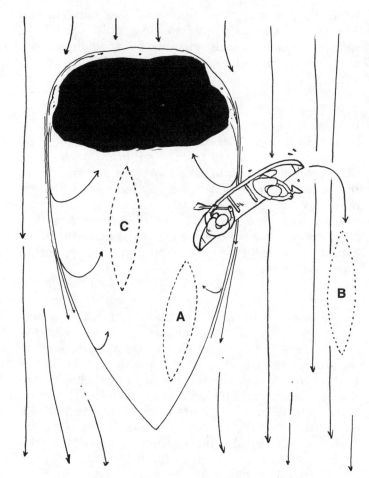

*The correct eddy position for a peel-out: boat **A** is near the back of the eddy, close to the eddy line. From here it can peel out to position **B** in the main current. Boat **C** is too close to the rock and too deep into the eddy to get the correct angle to leave. The boat should enter the main current at approximately a 45-degree angle. The paddler adds a stern pry to keep the boat from swinging around downstream too soon.*

up. Concentrate on the eddyline and that's where you'll end up.

There are some finer points of getting a good drive out of an eddy. One of these is to position the boat in the eddy so that you have enough room to build up speed. As always, you want to use the eddy current to help. Your position should be far enough back in the eddy to take at least a couple of forward strokes, without being so far back that you are in danger of floating out the back of the eddy. Keep in mind that this is a dynamic position. That is, if you are in the eddy, you won't be sitting still, you will be moving upstream toward the rock that created the eddy. The current in some eddies can be strong, and you can end up against the rock in short order. Not only will sitting sideways against a rock ruin your outgoing angle, you may have a problem getting far enough back in the eddy.

TIP: *Every corrective stroke is like stepping on the brakes. Try to get away from stepping on the gas and then standing on the brakes. Two suggestions for getting up speed quickly from a standing start: first, alternate forward and cross forward strokes, since these compensate somewhat for each other's tendency to turn the boat, and second, angle the boat toward your paddling side, so that those first few hard strokes turn you back the way you want to go. This is especially helpful when you're accelerating for a peel-out.*

—Ed Daugherty

The most advantageous position from which to peel out of an eddy is a compromise. If you start from the center of an eddy, you have a very good chance of ending up against the rock as you turn to go out in the current. A better position is usually one a bit closer to the eddyline. You don't want to get *too* close, however, because if the bow gets into the eddyline, the boat will spin around. Hugging the eddyline too closely also prevents you from having enough room to turn. The best position is somewhat to the side of the eddy, far enough inside to have room to set your angle.

Getting in and out of eddies requires practice, but it is an absolutely essential river skill. Start with large, slow eddies and gradually work your way up to small ones with abrupt eddy fences. Review the skill level guide in chapter 2.

Now let's look at the strokes needed to get in and out of eddies. For solo canoeists, eddies can be loosely grouped as on side or off side. Of the two, most paddlers have far more difficulty with the off-side ones. In tandem boats one paddler will be on side and the other off side, so it is simply a question of which one it will be.

For both eddy turns and peel-outs, the object is to cross the eddyline and *then* to turn. So in both maneuvers the first stroke is a forward stroke to build up momentum. A paddler needs to keep up this forward stroke until *after* his body crosses the eddyline or until he can comfortably reach over it. If he is in the main current, his object is to plant the paddle in the upstream current of the eddyline. If he is leaving an eddy, he plants it in the downstream current. He is interested in making use of current *differentials* here, so it does little good to plant the paddle in the same current that the boat is in. Instead he wants the countercurrent to help him turn the boat.

What strokes will a solo canoeist use when entering an eddy? Let's start with a right-handed paddler entering an on-side eddy. As our paddler approaches the eddy, he paddles forward, correcting as necessary, lining up the canoe at the correct 45-degree angle so that it will cross the eddyline high, right behind the rock that created it. Just as the bow starts to cross the eddyline, the paddler slides his paddle back along the gunnel and gives the boat a pry stroke. Why? Because otherwise the rejector line on the eddy will ride the bow down the eddyline and ruin his carefully set angle. Now the boat begins crossing the eddyline, and the paddler shifts his weight onto his right knee, leaning the boat into the turn (in this case, toward the rock). As his body crosses the eddyline, he reaches slightly forward, plants the paddle in the eddy, and assists the eddy in turning the boat by using a bow draw. As the boat swings around and the paddle approaches the boat, the paddler converts the draw into a forward stroke to bring the boat up into the eddy.

For a peel-out, the process is reversed. Starting a bit behind the rock and positioned near the eddyline, the paddler takes a couple of hard forward strokes, correcting as necessary to maintain his angle. He won't need to correct as he goes across the eddyline, but he will want to keep paddling forward as he does so. As the bow begins to cross the eddyline, he starts his weight shift, again onto his right knee. After his body clears the eddyline, he puts in another turning stroke (a bow draw or a stern pry), if needed, to turn the boat downstream. At the same time, he shifts his weight back over center. As you can see, there is nothing complicated about these strokes. In fact, it is possible to do the entire peel-out without using a single corrective stroke.

TIP: Try using a cross forward stroke to make small changes of direction when peeling out, rather than corrective strokes. This helps you keep your momentum up. If you must use a stern corrective stroke, a quick pry usually works best.

The off-side procedure is almost the same, except that the strokes are slightly different. Instead of an on-side bow draw, the paddler uses an off-side cross draw, which requires a somewhat surer sense of balance.

How about in tandem boats? The practice is much the same. Tandem canoes have an advantage in that the bow paddler crosses the eddyline early and so is able to initiate the turn sooner. The big disadvantage is that it is much harder to coordinate weight shifts with two people. Many tandem teams hedge their leans by having the sternman brace while the bowman draws. Let's see how this works with a bow-left–stern-right tandem canoe entering an eddy to their right side. Both paddlers use forward strokes approaching the eddy. As the bow crosses the eddyline, the bowman reaches across the boat and plants his blade *in the eddy*, forming a pivot for the canoe by using a cross bow draw. At the same time he shifts his weight onto his right knee. The sternman, meanwhile, puts in a quick pry just before hitting the eddyline, begins to shift his weight, and pushes the stern of the canoe around, using a reverse sweep. Since the sternman is already in a sweep position with the paddle out over the water, it's very easy for him to stabilize the canoe with a low brace by simply turning the blade's back face down. Some publications call this a sweeping low brace and recommend it as a matter of course. However, a better idea, unless a brace is really necessary, is for the sternman to keep paddling, driving the boat into the eddy. Meanwhile, the bowman converts his draw into a forward stroke, either cross or on-side, completing the eddy turn.

With the right- and left-handers' positions reversed, or for an eddy on the other side, the bowman would initiate the turn with an on-side draw just inside the eddy. The sternman would use a forward sweep to help with the turn and also to keep up the forward momentum. As the boat continues to turn, the sternman may follow the sweep with a stern draw (otherwise, as above, he keeps paddling). Turns on the sternman's off side do not allow him the option of a low brace, so any such stabilizing stroke must come from the bow. The sternman may, however, use a high brace.

Ferries

So far we've talked about getting in and out of eddies. Now it's time to introduce the third basic river maneuver: the ferry. Just as with river ferrymen of old, the object of the river ferry remains the same today—to get to the other side of the river without moving downstream. Combined with eddy turns and peel-outs, ferrying can be a very useful river skill in such situations as, for example, when you need to move above an obstacle or a rapid. Because most ferries begin in one eddy and end up in another, a ferry begins almost exactly like a peel-out. The only real difference is that in a peel-out the canoe turns downstream after leaving the eddy, but in a ferry the boat continues to point upstream, moving at an angle *across* the current. A ferry, more than any maneuver so far, requires the paddler to balance the forces of boat and river—the speed of the boat leaving the eddy and the force of the current moving downstream. We want the boat to move across the current, not downstream. If he simply powers the boat at a right angle to the current, he will end up downstream. If, however, he crosses the current at about a 45-degree angle, the boat can be made to move across the current without losing ground. The downstream current pushes against the side of the boat, sliding it along much as the wind propels a sailboat. The boat does, however, need some forward speed, both to get out of the eddy and to maintain its position in the current, which means that the paddler will have to continue paddling forward.

It should be easy to see that the critical part of the ferry is the angle. The ideal angle is about 45 degrees from upstream. More angle (the bow of the boat pointing more toward the opposite shore) and the boat slips downstream; less angle (the bow pointing more upstream) and the crossing speed slows. There are other

A tandem ferry. The boat has come out of the eddy on river left and heads across the current at a 45-degree angle. The stern paddler maintains the angle while the bow paddler keeps up the speed. Note the downstream lean of the boat.

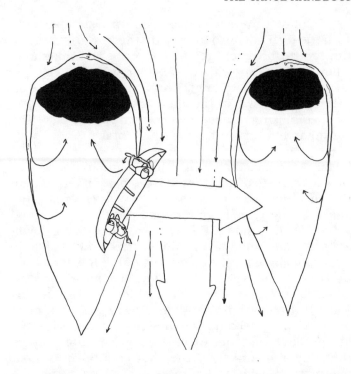

advanced techniques to enhance ferries, such as surfing across on a wave, but that's something for later (see chapter 6).

So much for theory. The tricky part of a ferry, especially in a canoe, is setting and maintaining the ferry angle. This angle must be set immediately upon leaving the eddy, held during the ferry, and then usually modified somewhat to enter the eddy on the other side. How? First, by driving out of the eddy as for a peel-out. In a ferry there's no time to brace, and speed in exiting the eddy is a must, as is setting the correct angle of exit. To say it another way, you can't expect to do a decent ferry if you can't do a good peel-out.

Weight shifts in a ferry are much the same as in a peel-out. Since the boat continues to move across the current, the paddler must shift his weight over his downstream knee and keep it there. When the boat enters the eddy at the other side of the ferry, however, the paddler must shift his weight back to the other knee.

THE STERN DRAW IN THE FERRY

The most effective stroke for maintaining the ferry angle on an on-side ferry is the stern draw. Why? Because it's easier to *pull* the stern around downstream than it is to *push* the bow back upstream with a sweep. The stern draw also integrates well with a forward stroke to maintain momentum.

In general, since it is easier to turn the boat downstream than upstream, it's often best to start a ferry with a bit too much upstream angle and let the current turn the boat down to the correct angle. If you start a ferry without enough upstream angle, it is very difficult to turn the boat back against the current.

As with most other things in canoeing, ferries can be divided into off-side and on-side. And as usual, the off-side moves are the more difficult. For an on-side ferry, the paddler's on side is downstream, which makes him feel a bit more secure. The on-side power strokes tend to turn the bow upstream, which helps to balance the force of the current trying to turn it downstream. The paddler may let the current turn the bow downstream for more ferry angle, or he may put in a quick pry. Turning the boat upstream is harder but still possible with forward sweeps or, more effective, with stern draws.

Off-side ferries are more difficult. The paddler now finds himself paddling on the upstream side of the boat. This not only makes it harder to brace if things go wrong, it also means that both the current and the necessary power strokes now tend to push the bow around downstream. Corrective strokes must be powerful, quick, and timely, and there is really only one corrective stroke—the stern pry—that works in swift water. For a successful off-side ferry, start with considerably more upstream angle than usual so that you can end up with the correct angle after the inevitable falloff downstream. Each power stroke must be followed with a powerful pry to keep the bow turned upstream, and you'd better have your weight shift right on this one, brother. Off-side ferries require practice to do well.

Tandem boats have a somewhat easier time of it, since the bowman can supply the forward power for ferries on either side, and the sternman can maintain the ferry angle. Generally, then, the bow paddler will keep up the speed with forward strokes while the stern paddler controls the boat's angle with a sweep or stern draw if his on side is downstream, or with a pry if it is upstream. It makes little sense for the bow paddler to try to steer.

FINISHING THAT FERRY

You're almost to the other side on a ferry, but the last ten feet . . . What a struggle! Look at the current differentials as you move from the middle of the river toward the shore. You are leaving fast water and entering slower water, with your bow entering the slow water first. When this happens, the fast water now pushes against the stern, which causes the boat to head up (upstream), which isn't a very good ferry angle to make shore. If you compound this by paddling on the downstream side, then your stroke also tends to head the boat upstream. Remember, you have to correct for both your stroke and the water. The solution is easy: As you approach your destination, just be paddling on the upstream side. Cross forward strokes here work just as well as forward ones. If you're dead set against switching sides and want to paddle on the downstream side, increase your angle to almost 90 degrees (perpendicular to the eddyline) when entering the slower eddy water. In really fast current, however, doing this will take you slightly downstream.

—Dave Moccia

Back Ferries

EVOLUTION OF THE BACK FERRY

The back ferry evolved as a technique for loaded tandem tripping canoes, and many tandem teams habitually back-ferried (they call it "setting") through the rapids. If a boat is in the main current and the paddlers want to generate a current differential, they must move the boat either faster or slower than the current. Properly done, paddling backward allows nearly as much control as moving forward. The paddlers could move more slowly downstream, cross the river to avoid obstacles and big waves, *and* see where they were going. A heavily laden tandem boat is less likely to swamp when paddled this way, since the bow has slightly more time to ride up a wave crest. Though back ferries are fairly straightforward for tandem boats, they are considerably harder in solo boats, but fun to develop for total boat control and playing.

Everything we've mentioned so far in this chapter can be done in reverse. This can be an interesting and rewarding exercise, but since the development of modern sport canoeing technique emphasizes aggressive forward paddling, your initial practice time is probably better spent in perfecting forward moves. With better water-reading techniques and more aggressive river tactics, the back ferry has fallen more into disuse, although it is still required for ACA canoe instructor certification.

The principle of the back ferry is exactly the same as that of the forward ferry, and the concepts of speed, angle, and lean still apply. From there on out, however, things are different. For starters, the pivot point of a solo boat is now forward of the paddler, making control more difficult. This is less of a problem with a tandem boat, but both suffer from the inability to see where they are going. Building up speed for maneuvers is also harder when the boat is moving backward.

For solo boats the first essential step in backferrying is to master the reverse strokes in the last chapter. For an on-side back ferry (that is, with the paddle on the downstream side of the boat), the paddler starts with an on-side back stroke, then continues to backstroke as the boat enters the current and begins the reverse ferry. To correct, he converts this back stroke into a sweep or bow rudder near the front of the boat (remember that we're working backward here).

The off-side back ferry is harder, and to do it correctly, you need to master the difficult cross back stroke. Starting in the eddy, begin with an on-side back stroke to get the boat moving. Then, as the boat crosses the eddyline, twist around into a cross back stroke. This keeps the blade on the downstream side of the boat, making correction easier. The cross back stroke, correctly executed, is powerful and works well for corrections. The first time you try this, however, you will probably feel like a Chinese puzzle. To adjust your ferry angle, slide the paddle forward into a cross draw or cross bow rudder. Dress warmly.

SIX

Intermediate Moving-Water Maneuvers

WE STARTED with basic strokes and water reading, and then put these together in fundamental river maneuvers (eddy turn, peel-out, and ferry). Building on that, we'll now combine these maneuvers into tactics for moving down the river.

But why bother with tactics? After all, a lot of people just crash their way down the river. There are a couple of reasons for having a plan. First, it's safer, since you have more control over what you're doing. But just as important, it's more fun, since it allows you to find some spots to play. Why are you on the river in the first place? To relax and float, to develop mastery of the boat, or just to say "I ran it"?

Finding Your Way

The bedrock river tactic is *eddy hopping*, that is, moving from eddy to eddy downstream (and sometimes upstream). Eddy hopping allows a paddler to break a section of river into smaller chunks. An eddy is a convenient place to stop—for a rest, to wait for another boat, or to scout what lies ahead—and allows paddlers to break their downstream momentum. The steeper a river, the more limited is the sight distance ahead. Blundering down the river into something you can't see is a sure recipe for disaster. Small sections, run one after another, are far easier to handle than a long section where difficulties come up too fast for the paddler to react. Once you enter a section like this, the increase in current (and hence boat) speed can be both dramatic and deceptive.

If you just want to slow down rather than stop completely, you can duck into the slack water behind a hole or into an eddy without making the upstream turn. This often allows enough time to plan your next move. If you do this behind a hole, however, don't get so close to the hole that the boat gets caught in the backwash.

In chapter 1 we discussed some simple methods of finding a route down the river. The two salient principles of route finding were to follow the deepest water, which is usually marked by downstream Vs and a wave train, and to avoid hazards. Now, to see how what we've learned so far fits together, let's go back to the rapid that we used as an example for basic water reading.

TIP: Scout from bottom to top. Although it's more convenient here to describe a rapid and the route through it from top to bottom, the way to scout and plan while on the river itself is the other way around: from bottom to top. With a complex rapid like the second one described here, the question is, "Where do I want to end up?" There may be plenty of great places to start, but probably not all of the resulting routes will end up where you want to go. It's like learning to shoot pool: you have to think three or four shots ahead. At the end of a section of river, you should be thinking how you are positioned for the next section, and the next.

At the top of our first hypothetical rapid are two boulders and a smooth tongue, followed by a series of tail waves. Behind each boulder is an eddy, and at the bottom is a small hole. If we can see all the way down the first drop, our tactic might be to catch one or both of the eddies behind the boulder. First, we would set up to cross the tongue and punch across the eddyline behind the rock. From here we can see the rest of the section below, including the size and location of the

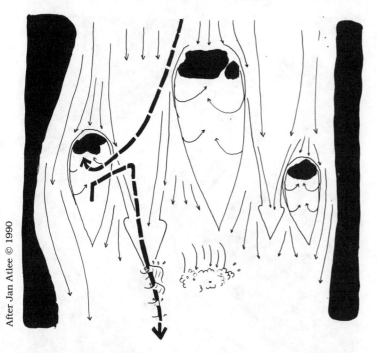

After Jan Atlee © 1990

River tactics 1: the paddler catches the eddy behind a rock, then peels out back into the main current to run the standing waves below.

hole. Since we're in the river-right eddy (remember, we always orient right and left facing downstream), it's a simple matter to peel out and stay to the right side of the current. But suppose we hadn't seen the hole and had caught the river-left eddy instead. A peel-out would land us squarely in the hole. To avoid this, we could ferry across the tongue of current to the other eddy and then peel out from there to head downstream. To make the ferry easier, we could use one of the waves (more on that in a moment).

Now let's look at the rapid shown on page 88. It's more complicated, with a lot more options. You see a horizon line for the first drop **A** and want to scout. After checking the route, you conclude that the best option is to catch the eddy behind the river-right boulder. This would let you see what's downstream. Below that are two hazards: a strainer on river left and a hole on river left center. The boulder in the right center is also a hazard, since it is capable of pinning a boat.

At **B** we have two options. The first is to peel out into the current coming down from **A** and run down the tongue between the boulder and the hole. The other,

River tactics 2: the paddler avoids the hydraulic by coming down the tongue on river right and catching the eddy below the boulder. When peeling out he may choose the route near the center of the river or near the right shore. To stop and to avoid the strainer, he eddies out in a shore eddy. From here he has several choices, either to keep to the inside of the bend (river left) and eddy out below the rocks or to run the waves or to skirt them on the right.

After Jan Atlee © 1990

and less desirable, is to ferry across the tongue of water coming through **A**, continue across the relatively slack water behind the first hole (being careful not to get too close) and go in front of the second hole, then turn and continue downstream near the river-left bank.

The first option is better in that it allows us to stay nearer to the river-right bank and thus to the inside of the bend. We also might consider catching the eddy behind the boulder at **C**, although we'd want to do it carefully if the tree extends very far into it. However, since water flows upstream in an eddy, we would be carried away from it. In the second option, we would immediately have to begin working our way toward the river-right bank after passing the hole, to avoid going into the undercut rock at **D**.

Below this, at **E**, is a large bank eddy on river right in which to collect ourselves. Because of the boulders below on river left, we would probably want to peel out of the eddy and continue down the center of the river, perhaps to catch a small eddy behind one of the boulders to scout the waves below. If the waves are runnable, we can blast straight through them. If not, we will have to skirt them to the left and head for the eddy on river left **F**. We might want to catch this eddy anyway, since these waves might be a great play spot for surfing.

GROUP TACTICS. So far we've considered only the actions of a single boat. How would a group handle a similar situation? As with any group, communication is the key. A group must maintain effective communication among all members, so that information about the river can be passed from back to front, and so that the leading members of the group don't continue downriver without knowing about a mishap at the back. The simplest way to exchange information is to stop periodically. This is no problem if the group is stopping anyway to scout, but otherwise it can be a drag. A better alternative is to develop a signaling system. Obviously, for this to work, boats must stay within sight of each other. The American Whitewater Affiliation (AWA) has developed a simple series of paddle signals that communicate basic concepts, such as "stop," "okay to continue," and which side of the river to proceed on.

Eddy hopping is also an essential technique for groups. Though a group of boats should stay close enough to be within sight of one another, they won't want to get so jammed together that they interfere with one another, or are unable to assist if something goes wrong. Spacing is important, and most times it works best for only one boat to move at a time, so that the group's attention is concentrated there in case something goes wrong. Stronger boats generally find the eddies first, then guide the weaker boats through, using river signals to control progress. Using a system like this can markedly speed a group's progress through a section of river.

SETUP AND BOAT POSITION
The phrase "it's all in the setup" is never more true than in canoeing. A good setup can make you look like a ballerina; a bad one, like a turkey. Say you are sliding down a tongue of water and want to end up on the right side. If you wait until you reach the bottom before turning, you've blown your chance. Set up ahead of time, starting a little left at the top, pointing right and driving that way as you come down.

Evaluating your boat position is always an ongoing process. If a bend in the river is turning right, the fast water and the waves will be on the outside of the turn. The wave train is a column of water comprising the peaks of the most prominent waves. There will be fast water directly on either side. If you start your run somewhere on the left side of the wave train, you can go left (outside) because the river wants to push you there. But to go right (inside), you have to paddle across and against all that current.

An easier setup is on the right side of the wave train. You can still go outside, but now your move to the inside is a piece of cake, since your boat is following a line right next to the slower water. The moral? Setting up on the inside of the waves in a bend gives you more options.

—Dave Moccia

Surfing

Surfing isn't just for the beach. River and ocean waves are practically identical, except that ocean waves move and river waves don't. You can surf a standing river wave much like an ocean wave. It's not just fun, it's a very useful technique for moving the boat around on the river. A crosscurrent ferry, for example, can be done practically without effort by using a convenient wave to surf from one eddy to another. Not all surfing is done on waves, however. Canoes front-surf or back-surf on waves, and side-surf in holes. All these variations use the same principles of strokes and water that we've already learned, and open the door to more paddling pleasure.

Breaking waves are fun, and just because they can swamp an open boat when hit head-on is no reason to avoid them. A good back stroke executed just before hitting the wave will lift the bow above the first wave, but what happens when there are more to come downstream and you have just killed your forward speed?

A better approach is to keep your momentum and quarter the wave or even hit it dead sideways. To keep from filling up, lean upstream just before you hit the breaking part. Present the hull to the crashing mass. When you hit it, lean back downstream. It helps here to have good outwales. Timing the lean and its duration is critical, and the move must be smooth and quick. A high brace on the downstream side—reach up and over the crest—is good insurance.

Surfin' USA! Gordon Grant shreds up a wave on the Nantahala. He has his weight shifted towards the stern to keep the bow up, and steers from the stern with either a pry or a stern draw.

FRONT SURFING. Wave surfing works by using gravity to cancel the river's downstream current, resulting in an equilibrium. When this is achieved, the boat, like the wave, stays in one place on the river. Surfing can be exciting. The river rushes past the boat, which seemingly ignores the laws of physics, floating over the flood. What is actually happening is this: the river's excess energy piles the water up, making the wave. In front and behind the wave is a *trough*, in which the water is depressed below its normal level. The *face* of the wave extends from the bottom of the trough to the *crest*, or top of the wave, and it is on the face that we surf. As the boat floats on the face of the wave, gravity pulls it down the face and, at some point, cancels out the current's downstream flow. The steeper the face, the faster the boat slides down it. If the face is not steep enough, or if the wave is not tall enough, the current pushes the boat over the crest and on downstream. If the wave is large and the face steep, the bow of the boat may bury into the trough or into the back of the wave ahead. Some of this depends on the design of the boat, and some on the length of the trough.

An ideal surfing wave, then, has a glassy smooth face, does not break at the top, and has a face steep enough to keep the boat on it but not so steep as to make the bow "pearl," or bury. The perfect wave also has convenient eddies on either side from which to enter. How do you find a wave like that? Usually by trying out a lot of them. Surfing, more than any technique we've mentioned so far, requires practice.

Let's go back for a moment to our first example of a rapid. We saw that it had eddies on either side and a train of waves in between. Let's now use one of these waves to assist in a ferry. We start with a solo boat in the river-right eddy, with a right-handed paddler. The paddler begins his approach as if to do a normal ferry, setting his exit angle from the eddy at 45 degrees. This time, however, he crosses the eddyline to put the bow of the boat into the trough of the wave. As the boat crosses the eddyline, he shifts his weight downstream, but as the bow enters the trough, the force of gravity now begins to pull the boat down into the trough. If the wave is right (and we'll assume that this one

THE CROSS HIGH BRACE

You're floating sideways into a big wave or hole with your paddle on the upstream side. Your boat starts to flip upstream. A low brace on the upstream side is not only ineffective but actually aids the river in its attempt to dunk you.

Instead, hit the hole with your paddle on the upstream side. As your boat starts to flip upstream, shift your upper body weight over the downstream gunnel. To keep from falling in, you land on a *cross high brace* and recover.

The cross high brace starts with upper body rotation to your off side. The paddle position is much like a cross bow draw, except that the T-grip hand is higher (head level) and the shaft hand is almost directly under it. The paddle shaft is almost vertical. The blade is as far from the boat as is comfortably possible.

To recover, pull the shaft into your hips pushing out a little on the T-grip. Then pull your head into the center of the boat, shifting your weight downstream. Just the brace position, without recovery, can often be very effective for surfing holes and riding out wave trains. In these circumstances just a little pressure on the paddle blade is all the extra balance you'll need to have a good ride.

TURNING WITH WAVES

Smaller breaking waves and holes can help turn your boat. Hit them perpendicular and you will go through straight. Hit them with a little angle and they will surf you right or left.

If a breaking wave or hole is guarding the entrance to an eddy, so much the better. Drop the front third of your boat into it almost dead sideways, point just a little downstream and lean into the turn. The backwash will grab the bow, taking the place of your paddle plant. The downstream current will whip your stern around, and your lean will turn the boat into the eddy, leading to a successful eddy turn with no strokes. But be sure to set up and have forward momentum.

Turning your canoe is easier if the bow is out of the water, in the air. Start your turning stroke as the bow approaches the peak of a wave. To turn left, lean right. This really helps boats with a lot of **V** in the hull.

—*Dave Moccia*

is), gravity pulls the boat down the face of the wave and keeps the boat from going downstream. A forward stroke from the paddle causes the boat to slide sideways in the direction it is pointing, as if it were on ice. Very little paddle force is required, and the effect is amazing, especially if you have been struggling with ferries before. The boat comes out of the eddy and rockets across the current almost with a will of its own. (Canoe instructors like to show off with this technique, demonstrating a ferry in one or two strokes.)

Entering the eddy on the other side of the river as you ferry across is sometimes a problem. Here we face the same problems as before with crossing the eddyline and being pushed away by the rejector line. Thus a boat crossing the trough at the ideal 45-degree angle sometimes bounces off the far eddyline, turns upstream, and begins surfing the wave. Once this happens, it's often hard to regain enough momentum to break through the eddyline. The solution is to let the boat's angle fall off downstream somewhat as it approaches the eddy, so that it hits the eddyline closer to the perpendicular, thereby punching across (see Finishing That Ferry, in chapter 5).

Surfing is also fun for its own sake. Shredding a wave is one of the most fun things you can do in a canoe. Watch a good canoeist surf sometime—it is a concerto of river, paddle, and the invisible forces of gravity working together. Getting on the wave is much the same as for a ferry. Exit the adjoining eddy so that the bow enters the trough of the wave. You may have to give it a couple of tries to find exactly where the bow needs to be to get the boat on the face of the wave. This varies somewhat from wave to wave and boat to boat. Practice a few times by ferrying back and forth. The object in surfing is to get the boat turned upstream perpendicular to the wave so that it stops sliding across the face of the wave and stays in one place. You'll find that the wave is like ice, and once you start across, it's hard to stop. One of two things usually happens: either the paddler approaches the wave pointed too far upstream and the boat stalls on the eddyline facing upstream, or he goes zipping across the wave in a ferry, unable to stop. What is needed is a quick, positive way to turn the boat out of the ferry and onto the wave when you get to the right spot.

A surfing ferry. Gravity pulls the boat down in the trough of the wave and keeps the boat from slipping backwards, while the paddler controls the boat's angle with a stern pry or stern draw.

Remember that the correct ferry angle is about 45 degrees (upstream here is 0 degrees), but also that it's easier to turn the boat downstream than upstream. Thus it's often better to start with the boat pointed slightly too far upstream, letting it fall off downstream until you get the angle you want. Same thing here. To surf, set an angle of 20 or 30 degrees from upstream, so that you won't have to turn the boat upstream to stabilize it on the wave. You want the boat to break through the eddyline and move slowly across the wave, then stop. Your control over this cross-wave speed is the boat's upstream angle. More angle equals more speed, and no angle (that is, facing straight upstream) equals no speed. Once on the face you need only steer, since gravity will hold the boat in place.

Steering requires a light touch. Most paddlers begin by overcorrecting, first letting the boat's angle fall off too much and then cranking in too much compensation. The most important consideration about steering, however, is to do it *from the stern*. The bow is partly buried in the back of the next wave in front. This makes it hard to turn, and bow strokes, like draws, are almost useless. The stern, on the other hand, sticks into the air and so is relatively easy to swing around. The farther sternward you put your strokes, the less effort steering will be. The most effective strokes are prys to turn the boat to the paddler's on side, and stern draws to turn the boat to the off side. Many paddlers try to turn the boat to their off side by making forward sweeps. These, since they have most of their effect forward of the pivot point, are much less effective than the stern draw, which operates behind the pivot point. Think of the bow as being relatively fixed in the trough, then plant the paddle and pull the stern toward you to straighten the boat on the wave. Reaching back for stern draws and pries not only increases their effectiveness by moving them farther from the pivot point, it also has the beneficial effect of shifting the paddler's weight backward, unloading the bow and making steering easier.

A surfing sequence works something like this: the paddler goes out on a wave as if for an on-side ferry (his paddle is on the downstream side of the boat). As he crosses the eddyline, he shifts his weight to his right knee. Since the boat will ride on the tilted face of the wave, he needs to shift his weight slightly more than when just crossing the current. As the boat crosses the eddyline, the bow enters the trough of the wave, and the boat begins to slide across the face. Maintaining just enough angle to keep the boat moving, he moves across the wave, then does a quick stern draw to pull the stern around and get the bow facing upstream. From here on out it's funhog city. Our paddler now shifts his weight backward to lighten the bow as much as possible, and controls his angle by alternately prying and stern drawing. If he lets the angle fall off, he will begin moving to one side or the other, and can stop again with a quick corrective stroke.

To surf a wave from an off-side ferry, the situation is reversed, and the initial correction to stabilize the boat on the wave's face is the pry.

Tandem boats operate similarly, but as always there are some differences. For starters, the weight of the bow paddler makes the front of a tandem boat sink deeper into the trough. This means that the bowman's strokes will be largely ineffective for steering, so his efforts are better spent providing the power to get the boat on the wave. Once there, the sternman steers, using the same prys and stern draws as the solo paddler. The bowman, meanwhile, may amuse himself by doing stunts like paddle twirls and headstands.

A word or two about weight shifts is appropriate here, since surfing is where a lot of paddlers experience the true meaning of the term *windowshaded*.

The steeper the wave, the more the paddler must lean the boat (and shift his weight) downstream into the wave. In surfing, even more than in eddy turns, the need for weight shifts is often virtually instantaneous. In our last illustration, for example, the solo paddler must have his weight on his right knee when moving across the wave to the right, but when the boat turns upstream, he must quickly center his weight. If he overcorrects and the boat then starts to turn to the left on the wave, he must swiftly shift his weight onto his left knee. The results of tardy weight shifts are abrupt.

All waves are not created equal, nor are most of them uniform all the way across. Just as some waves are better for surfing than others, there is usually one spot on a wave that's a better surf site than the rest. Some paddlers call this the sweet spot, and very often the best move is to ferry over to it and stop. Once there, you may find that the boat stays there on its own, allowing you to show off with paddle twirls and tosses.

To get off the wave, the paddler either goes into an eddy on the side, or simply pushes back off the face of the wave to continue downstream.

BACK SURFING. It's not quite true to say that back surfing is the exact opposite of front surfing. In some ways it's actually easier once you get on the wave.

Most waves have a "sweet spot" where the boat will stay with little help from the paddler. It's a good place to show off.

Most solo boats have a slight sternward weight bias, and this tends to make the boat slide down the face of the wave faster. To get into a back surf, you first need to learn the back strokes discussed in chapter 4, then try some reverse eddy turns and ferries to get warmed up (or cooled down, if you blow it).

When you're going out on the wave, think backward. Now it's the *stern* that's going to be buried, so you need to steer from the bow and swing it around to stabilize on the wave. All those back strokes like stern prys and stern draws won't work, and you'll need to use forward-oriented strokes like bow draws and prys to keep the boat straight. For the same reason, you need to lean toward the bow both to get some of the weight off the stern and to get the paddle forward. Otherwise everything works pretty much the same. Like back strokes, however, this is a technique that might better be left until you've mastered front surfing.

Side Surfing

Although the name makes it sound like wave surfing, side surfing is a very different thing. Front and back surfing are done on the face of a wave; side surfing takes place in a hole. Small holes are great fun to play in, and they sharpen useful skills like body lean. Getting in and—more important—getting out of a hole are skills you'll want to have on the river, since there are times when you may find yourself inadvertently sitting in a hole that you'd rather not be in. This doesn't have to end in disaster or humiliation if you know how to handle it.

Let's review the two varieties of holes: the breaking hole, in which a wave breaks back upstream, and the hydraulic, in which there is actually an upstream current. Each one causes a depression in the water in which the boat sits, and both work for side surfing. The best bet for starting out, however, is to find a *small* hydraulic. Even a tiny one, barely big enough to accommodate the boat, has surprising power. It will give you, among other things, some appreciation of what it's like to be in a big one. Watch someone else first: most popular rivers have well-defined play spots, and these are often good places to start. But know whom you're watching. An expert may make it *look* easy, but that doesn't mean it really is. Like a surfing wave, a good play hole has eddies on either side so that you can get into it easily and have some place to go afterward.

You can ferry across a hole just as you can across a wave, except that a hole isn't as slick. Ferrying across the hole is often a good way to start. In fact, you may find that, despite your best efforts, the hole whisks you out the other end, and you have to take a back stroke to stop.

The key to side surfing is balance, which is different from balance in wave surfing: you have to keep your weight shifted the entire time you're in the hole. The tricky parts are entering and exiting. Entering a hole is pretty much the same as setting up for a ferry on a wave. You want to aim the bow into the hole's depression and then paddle forward into it. Unlike a wave, the hole will guide you in. At first, go in with your paddle on the downstream side of the hole. Paddle forward and shift your weight onto your downstream knee, leaning the boat up and away from the water coming over the obstacle. Too much initial boat lean is better than not enough, and you can stabilize yourself with a low brace.

Remember, however, that the object is to find the balance point in order to sit more or less upright in the hole. The *boat* is tilted downstream with the paddler's weight on his downstream knee. As in a peel-out, a paddler avoids putting his weight on the paddle and hanging out over the gunnel.

Once in the hole, you will notice another big difference between this and a wave—it's bouncy in there! The energy in most holes alternately builds and breaks, tossing the boat around like a load of clothes. There are more holes named Washing Machine than you would probably care to count.

Now experiment. Let the boat tilt back toward the horizontal a bit. At a certain point the upstream edge will begin to catch as the water starts to jerk on the edge of the boat. Not enough lean. There is an obvious difference between the two motions: the normal bouncing of the boat, which is an up-and-down and back-and-forth motion, and the yanking of the water on the upstream gunnel, which wants to flip the boat upstream. The first is normal, fun, and unavoidable; the second can be cured by leaning the hull downstream a bit more. The balance point is usually just before you reach the upstream catch point. Once you feel comfortable with just being stable in a hole, experiment to find the balance point. Ideally, you should be able to balance without using the paddle at all. Try some paddle twirls! Thigh straps (see chapter 9 for more details) definitely help, since they keep your upstream knee down on the hull and allow you to hang your weight against them toward the downstream side of the boat.

Once you've found the balance point, dealing with holes gets much easier. No longer do you have to use your paddle solely for support. Now you can use it for moving back and forth in the hole. This makes getting out of a hole much easier, because the only good way to get out of a hole is to slide out the ends. Some publications advise you to reach over the reverse current to pull yourself downstream, but this requires you to pull yourself both up (out of the depression) and upstream past the reverse current—a difficult thing to do even in a small hole. Moving sideways, however, is easy. After

Hole surfing. Bob Powell shows that if you're good, you don't need a paddle. His weight is over the boat on his left (downstream) knee, with the hull tilted slightly downstream.

you've gained some confidence balancing in a small hole, try moving back and forth, using forward strokes and back strokes. This happens naturally to some extent anyway: even if you just sit there, the water will move you in one direction or another, often alternately back and forth. As always, you want to work with the water, so time your strokes to coincide with the natural motion of the boat.

Exiting a hole is one circumstance in which a back stroke is definitely better than a forward stroke. In a canoe, a reverse stroke or sweep, done properly with the torso, is a very powerful move—more so than a forward stroke. As a result, backing out of a hole is often more effective than trying to paddle out forward. Here again the natural motion of the hole can help. If you are unable to get out, try going back and forth along the hole to develop a rocking motion, using it to help build the momentum to break free.

The transition from the hole's backwash into the current can also be awkward. As the boat backs out of the hole, the pull on the upstream edge gradually becomes less—until the end of the boat gets back into the current, at which time it suddenly picks up again. This often leads to a flip, so when coming out of a hole, be ready for this transition.

Hole surfing is great fun, as well as being a valuable skill builder. After surfing a few holes, you'll wonder why you ever had trouble with eddy turns and peel-outs.

By now we've put together a basic skills package for the river. The very basics of canoeing are the simple skills—eddy turns, peel-outs, and ferries—whose mastery is essential. Work toward more advanced skills like surfing, but use them to help you perfect the basics. Too many paddlers insist on slopping through the elementary but essential first steps in the quest for adrenaline. We'll have more to say about that in the chapter on safety.

SEVEN

The Open-Canoe Eskimo Roll

By Nolan Whitesell

ROLLING AN OPEN CANOE has long been considered an interesting but mostly useless stunt. I've often heard people ask about rolling, "What good is it? What are you gonna do with a canoe full of three tons of water?" More and more canoeists are learning, however, that rolling an open boat is practical and even easy, as well as a lot more fun than swimming. And learning the roll described here will improve your ability to brace—meaning that you'll have to roll less often anyway. Knowing you can roll up if you do flip will totally change your outlook on the sport. When scouting, you'll look at the runout below a rapid and know that if you get flipped by that big curling wave, you'll be back in control well before your friend has even reached for the throw bag. If you think you were excited the first time your low brace saved you on the river, hold on to your helmet—the roll's gonna blow your mind!

You don't need brawn to roll a canoe: you need technique. Consequently, I've found that women tend to learn faster and more easily than most men. Macho males often try muscling it up rather than concentrating on the move and their balance. As a 110-pound woman wrote me recently about learning to roll, "It was like learning to ride a bike; what had seemed impossible moments before became simple with the right motions and balance. It's not really tough at all."

Proper outfitting is essential for rolling an open canoe. The tighter you are locked to the boat, the more your critical body motion can be transferred to the canoe for an effective roll. You need solid contact at the knees, thighs, and feet. The best outfitting for rolling an open canoe is a saddle with foot braces (while kneeling in the saddle, you press your toes or the ball of your foot back against the foot brace), or a pedestal with snug thigh straps and foot braces. In addition to holding you tightly, your outfitting system must allow you to get out easily whenever you want.

Preparation

When learning to roll, try to do away with any distractions in your learning environment. If possible, find warm water to practice in—preferably a pool or lake where the water's not moving. Trying to learn in ice-cold water is difficult, especially when it's washing you downstream. If you feel comfortable doing so, take off your life jacket when practicing. Practicing without it is less constricting and you more easily feel what your body is doing.

If you find it difficult to concentrate with water percolating up your nose, take a diving mask to your practice sessions. The mask will help you get a clear picture of what's happening underwater. If you don't have a diving mask, swimming goggles and nose plugs make a good substitute—and fit in your pocket more easily.

Don't go out alone to practice; have someone else there to help. Start by turning the boat over and practicing coming out of the boat in a wet exit. You should have absolutely no concern about leaving your boat whenever necessary. Just knowing that you won't be trapped under the canoe will relieve much anxiety.

The Low-Brace Roll

Although the low-brace roll described here is not the only way to roll a canoe, I have found that it works best for beginning rollers. Later you may want to try variations to see what effect they have, but trying to imitate someone you see on the river is usually not a good idea. Some people who can roll successfully because they have the timing and the basic motion also have bad habits that you don't want to copy when you're learning.

INITIATION. Your body rights the canoe; your arms do not. When you turn your canoe over, the muscles of your abdomen, back, and lower body are what roll it back into place underneath you. The main function of the paddle is to provide some leverage to help you carry out the correct body motion.

To practice the motion that is the essence of the roll, sit comfortably locked into the boat and have a helper stand in waist-deep water next to you. Your helper can hold your paddle blade in one hand and the nine- or ten-foot painters attached to your canoe's bow and stern in the other. Put your paddle straight out on your most comfortable paddling side. Float the paddle on the surface perpendicular to the boat, and hold the T-grip on the outside of the gunnel. The palm of the hand holding the T-grip is facing up and the thumb of that hand is facing forward. Leave your other hand off the paddle for now. During the following move, have your friend hold the blade of the paddle firmly and keep it on or near the surface while still allowing it to move laterally across the surface. Now put your mask on, take a couple of deep breaths, and lean over to that side until the boat rolls upside down. Your T-grip hand is still facing palm up, thumb forward. The paddle blade is still floating.

An easy way to learn. A helper holds the bow and stern lines to keep the boat from yawing away from him as you begin the hip snap. When you're ready to practice a full roll . . .
(Photo: Dan McClure)

the assistant can make sure the paddle is in a good starting position and then stand by in case you don't come up. Here the roll worked. (Photo: Dan McClure)

Stop here for a moment to look around at the boat, your position, the surface, and the paddle. It is important to have a clear picture of these in your mind.

Now twist your torso up to the surface of the water so that you can reach up with your shaft hand and grab the paddle shaft where you normally would. Push your head up toward the surface as much as possible. This is the windup move, which stores energy as in a spring. The more you can stretch up toward the surface, the more momentum you'll have when you release the spring. If you can't reach all the way to the surface (and you probably won't be able to), pull the shaft down far enough that you can press the mask or your forehead against the back of your shaft hand; your face, shoulders, and chest should face the bottom of the pool.

To turn the canoe back over, push down hard with your head and lift up with your on-side knee. (If you floated the paddle on the right side of the canoe, your right knee is your on-side knee.) Now you are releasing the energy stored in the spring. This motion is the essence of the roll. Don't use your arms. Keep your forehead pressed to your shaft hand as though it were glued in place.

Practice the motion repeatedly. With your helper holding the blade just out of the water, keep your head cemented to the shaft hand and practice pivoting the canoe up over you and then back down under you, using your torso and lower body muscles. Your body needs to get the message that your arms don't roll the canoe.

Once you understand the basic move, put some oomph into it. When you're lifting up hard on the on-side knee, push down with the off-side knee. Try for a fast pop. Never take your forehead off the back of your shaft hand. Keeping it there forces you to push down on the paddle with your head instead of trying to push yourself up off the paddle with your arms. Pushing with your arms is ineffective because it raises your center of gravity before your torso and lower body have had a chance to right the canoe beneath you. It also makes you susceptible to a shoulder dislocation. Remember, you're trying to center your body over a canoe that's just been turned upright. If you don't succeed, you won't come up—at least not consistently and safely.

FINISHING THE ROLL. The lower body rotation is what turns the canoe almost all the way upright. Finishing the roll is a matter of centering your body over the nearly upright canoe.

To do this, slide your head back along the shaft past your T-grip hand and into the belly of the boat. Move your head across the boat and don't start pulling up until you're all the way to the opposite side of the canoe. The movement of your head centers your weight and continues the turning momentum initiated by your lower-body rotation.

PUTTING IT ALL TOGETHER. Although the roll is one continuous motion, we'll break it down here into separate steps for clarity.

• Float your paddle out to the side of the canoe on your usual paddling side. Hold the T-grip with your palm up and your thumb forward.

• Tip over toward your on side.

• Reach your head up toward the paddle floating on the surface.

• Grab the paddle shaft and get your forehead on top of your shaft hand, turning your face, shoulders, and chest to face the bottom of the river.

• Push down with your head against the paddle shaft, lift up with your on-side knee, and push down

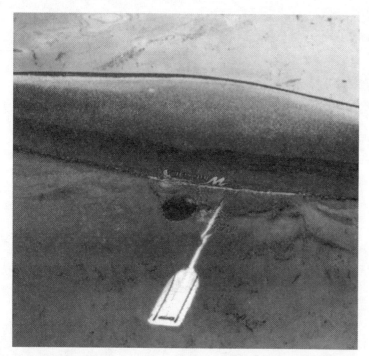

Float the paddle out to the side on your strong paddling side and then tip over toward your paddle. Reach up with your shaft hand and grab the paddle where you normally would. Reach your head up toward the surface and place your forehead on the back of the shaft hand. This is like winding up the spring. (Photo: Dan McClure)

Push down with your head. Lift up with your on-side knee (the side you floated the paddle on) and push down with your off-side knee. This is like releasing the spring. Your torso and lower body are what right the canoe—don't try to push yourself up with your arms. (Photo: Dan McClure)

As the canoe turns back underneath you, continue pushing down with your head and lifting with the knee. Stay with it. (Photo: Dan McClure)

When the canoe is nearly upright, slide your head along the paddle shaft toward the off-side gunnel. This will continue the turning momentum begun by your lower body. (Photo: Dan McClure)

Raise your head only after your weight is centered over the upright canoe. (Photo: Dan McClure)

with your off-side knee. Keep pushing down with your head until the canoe is nearly upright.

• Slide your head back along the shaft, past the T-grip and into the belly of the canoe. Don't lift your head until it has reached the opposite gunnel and the canoe is upright.

COMMON FAULTS.

• Lifting your head away from the paddle shaft too soon and trying to push yourself up with your arms (the movement you use when pushing away from a table and standing up).

• Not sliding your head back across the paddle shaft to center your body at the end of the roll.

• Lifting your head too soon.

Once you can right the canoe with a helper holding the paddle blade, have your helper provide less and less resistance to the paddle until he can actually let go immediately after your windup. Now practice on your own with your helper standing nearby. Don't concentrate on getting your head out of the water; focus instead on the motion of pushing your head down,

Seen from underwater, notice how the head stays down on the paddle shaft while the canoe is being rolled upright. (Photo: Dan McClure)

lifting your on-side knee and pushing down with your off-side knee. Your friend can help you if you don't come up.

Do short, focused practice sessions and then quit before you're tired and frustrated. Otherwise, you'll learn bad habits. Practice only good, effective rolls, and realize that you're using different muscles. Once you get the right motion, think about it from time to time as you go about your week. Just picturing it in your head will help you improve.

Once you've done a roll successfully on one side and have practiced it several times, take another good look at what's happening underwater. Use your mask to look at the boat, the surface, your paddle, and your body position. Your first few unplanned rolls in turbulent water on the river will probably feel very disorienting: having a clear mental image on file will help.

Before you convince yourself that you can only roll on one side, start working on your off-side roll. Having mastered a roll on each side is very useful. Initially, as you are perfecting the efficiency of your roll, you may need to switch to the downstream side to roll up. As your roll gets more efficient, you will find it much safer to roll on the upstream side, because an inopportune

CANOE DESIGN

It is impossible to talk about the open canoe roll without at least touching on canoe design. Every canoe can be rolled, but variations in design affect how easily (and therefore how reliably) it can be done. The best advice regarding any canoe is to try it first, but you don't actually have to know how to roll a canoe to test for rollability. Put the canoe in the water and lean it. It should feel stable. Lean it farther and let in a few gallons of water to simulate the actual conditions. Take a few strokes. It should feel stable and controllable. Leaning the boat with water in it tells you how easily it will roll.

—*Nolan Whitesell*

rock just under the surface during a downstream roll may jam you, but the same hit during an upstream roll will merely assist your motion toward the surface.

One of the sweetest advantages open canoes have over decked boats is that wonderful open belly in front of the seat. When you find yourself upside-down in rocky water, you need only lean up into that protective turtle shell—head, shoulders, and arms can be completely protected. (Surprisingly, there is usually even a trapped air pocket to breathe from.) Your back is protected by your life jacket, so it is much more reasonable to hang in there and wait for deeper water to roll. This is a good reason to keep your canoe open in front of where you sit. Lay the blade of your paddle upon the bow of the canoe or just off to the side, so that the paddle is lying along the long axis of the boat.

This tucked position is similar to that used by kayakers. It's also similar to the tuck that used to be taught for the high-brace roll in a solo decked canoe. Starting from the tuck, this high-brace roll involved sweeping the paddle out to the side of the canoe, much like a kayak sweep roll, and then turning the paddle over to initiate the roll.

I discourage this type of high-brace roll for a couple of reasons. It's much more conducive to shoulder dislocation than the low-brace roll, which keeps the elbows in close. Also, when you flip a canoe, it's often not necessary or desirable to take the time to go through the routine of tucking and setting up before you roll. With a low-brace roll, you just maneuver the blade back to the surface if it's not already there, then roll up.

If you're in turbulent or rocky water when you flip and you know you're not about to pin on a rock, you might want to tuck forward and wait to reach a calmer place to roll. When you do sweep your body out to the side of the canoe to roll up, don't worry about doing anything fancy with your paddle on the way; just position it so that it's at a right angle to the centerline of the canoe, as described earlier, and then roll.

The roll I've described is basically a glorified low brace. Most of the time you won't need to roll if you can do a good low brace. When you feel yourself flipping,

Tucking

simply push your head and body (protected behind the paddle shaft) down against the paddle shaft and lift with your on-side knee to get the boat back upright, then pull your weight back in and across the canoe. *The head is the key.* Don't try to lift your head up and away from your paddle until the canoe is fully upright and you have centered your weight over the boat.

Rolling a canoe looks complicated in print and may seem mysterious the first time you try it. So did your first try on a bicycle. But learning to roll is the same as riding that bike—once you get the timing and balance put together, it will be simple.

EIGHT

Directions

CANOEING IS an extraordinarily varied sport: one in which it really is possible to have it all. With equal enjoyment you can paddle the quiet black waters of a Florida swamp or run the white thunder of a rapidly dropping mountain river. Build a solid base of skills first—that's what this book is about. Then start looking for directions. On white water you can do some pretty fancy stuff, from hot dogging to slalom racing. On flat water you can take up tripping, freestyle paddling, or racing.

White Water

Two of the biggest trends in whitewater canoesport are the increased use of solo canoes and the technique of rolling open canoes. Solo canoes continue to get smaller (one manufacturer recently introduced an eleven-foot model) and outfitting options get more sophisticated every year. Open canoes have continued to invade water once reserved for decked boats, and have blown to atoms the old saw about canoes being suitable only for Classes II and III water.

PLAYING AND HOT DOGGING. Playing in an open boat is the start of a transition from survival to ballet. It is soothing to the spirit and—when you're concentrating on yourself, the boat, and the river—a form of meditation. Playing sharpens the reflexes and increases the skill level. The more you play, the less you have to think about how individual strokes affect your boat. All of a sudden you forget the strokes, since they have become second nature. Now you look at where you want to go and you're there. Everything is smooth and efficient, and paddling becomes a dance. This dance comes in two varieties: playing, which is done for your own enjoyment, and hot dogging, which is usually performed before an audience to appease your ego. Hot dogging tends to work your timing and balance a bit more, and wearing a helmet is a good idea.

There are many forms of playing and hot dogging. Here are a few suggestions from Dave Moccia:

• *Playing*: Surf a wave or hole facing upstream. *Hot dogging*: Back-surf the same wave using your cross bow pry and cross bow draw to steer—or stand on your head in the boat!

• *Playing*: Surf a hole sideways on a low or high brace. *Hot dogging*: Exchange boats—or stack boats on top of each other while surfing. Or do any of the above sitting on your flotation, feet on a thwart, or standing, or standing on the gunnels.

• *Playing*: Eddy-hop through a rapid using cool and poise. *Hot Dogging*: Eddy backward, or hit eddies so tight that three feet of your stern hangs over the drop.

• *Playing*: Practice your braces and let a little water pour in each time, or practice your balance by leaning your boat and steadily holding your gunnel a half inch above the water for fifteen seconds with your paddle out of the water. *Hot dogging*: Roll your canoe in front of a beginning kayak clinic.

• *Playing*: Do 360-degree spins in recirculating holes. *Hot dogging*: Add paddle twirls and occasionally stand up.

• *Playing*: Make the moves any kayak can make. *Hot dogging*: Make the moves the good and crazy kayakers make.

• *Playing*: Stand up under low bridges. *Hot dogging*: Do the same but throw your paddle over the bridge and catch it on the other side.

• *Playing*: Do S-turns with the least number of strokes, concentrating on speed, angle, and lean. *Hot dogging*: Do them backward, standing up. Or find a fast, narrow jet of water with good eddies on both sides for a dynamic S-turn. First take all the flotation and gear out of your boat to make it as light as possible— your bow should be out of the water about one and a half feet. Peel out. When entering the eddy on the other side, see how high you can lift your bow. With a little practice you can easily get enough altitude to land on another boat. Double points if your aim is good enough to center your bow on a tandem canoe.

• *Playing*: Be loose at the hips and float sideways through a run of standing waves, rocking back and forth—don't use your paddle, but rely only on your balance, the timing of your leans, and the movement of your hips. Or find a slow, flat stretch and close your eyes for five strokes or so, then see whether you have stayed on course. Try to feel when to use the corrective strokes. *Hot dogging*: Sit in an eddy in a fast chute and ferry or peel out in front of rafts, seeing how close you can come without getting run over—goofy thrills for you and the rafters. Make sure there is plenty of run-out and nothing to jeopardize the raft (like a raft-flipping wave) in case they try to avoid you.

The most important thing about playing and hot dogging, Moccia says, is to smile. That way, even if you mess up, it will look like you meant to do it!

RACING. If you're looking for a way to work out and improve your paddling as well as have some fun, try racing. Time that you spend paddling gates in moving water will be well rewarded, since it will force you to refine both your water-reading skills and your paddling technique. Even more important, one of the basic concepts of racing is learning to plan and execute a series of moves down a course.

Slalom racing was developed to simulate a river with rocks and eddies. Instead of hauling boulders around, however, race-course designers hang colored poles, called gates, over the river on a crosspiece. A typical slalom race course consists of twelve to twenty-five numbered gates scattered along a section of river no longer than six hundred meters. The gates must be negotiated in sequence from the upstream side (marked by a pair of red-and-white poles) or the downstream side (green-and-white poles).

Scoring in the slalom depends on two factors: the speed with which the boat completes the course, expressed as seconds of elapsed time, and additional time in the form of penalty points. Touching a gate adds ten seconds to your time. Missing a gate entirely, flipping in it, or passing through it in the wrong direction adds fifty seconds. The winner is the paddler with the lowest score. The difficulty of the course varies greatly with the level of competition: a national championship will be more challenging than a club race.

Open canoe slalom is generally divided into tandem and solo classes according to the length and style of the boat. A race boat tends to be radical, unforgiving, and fast. It may be an expensive, hand-built model made of Kevlar and exotic composites, and weighing about half what a normal play boat would.

If you'd like to try slalom without a lot of expense and commitment, enter a citizens' slalom or a regional series. These have become popular in the East, and have served to get a broader base of participants into racing. Citizens' slaloms, as the name implies, are simplified versions of standard slalom races, with the rules adjusted for touring equipment (and paddlers). No real race boats (or real racers) are permitted, and all the gates are fairly basic. Try it and have fun.

The other main variation of competition is downriver, or wild-water, racing. Here the object is simple: to get down a given section of river in as little time as possible. In this it is similar to marathon racing, ex-

Radical moves and radical boats characterize today's open-canoe slalom racing. (Photo: Mad River Canoe)

Downriver, or wildwater racing, puts skinny boats down the river in the shortest possible time. (Photo: Mad River Canoe)

cept that the wild-water racer has the additional complication of rapids to contend with. Downriver boats are long and slender, with higher sides and slightly more fullness in the bow than their flatwater cousins.

DECKED BOATS. There's no getting around it. No matter how careful you are, a boat with an open top will take on some water in a rapid. One obvious way to circumvent this is to put a deck on top. Another is to fill the boat with flotation. Some of today's whitewater boats are so stuffed that they are virtually decked. Real decking ranges from a fabric spray cover on an open canoe to a deck designed as part of the boat. Once the deck becomes a continuation of the hull, the shape of the canoe begins to change radically, enough so that the name of the boat changes also. From here on they are "C-boats": C-1s (solo decked canoes) and C-2s (tandem decked canoes). These boats began to assume their present shape in the early seventies, when the international racing rules finally allowed the bow and stern of a canoe to be lower than the cockpit.

All C-1s and C-2s require the paddler to kneel, which can be painful for those accustomed to paddling from a seated position. In a C-1, the paddler usually sits on a foam pedestal or a wooden thwart, holding himself in with thigh straps. A spray skirt of neoprene or coated nylon fits over a round cockpit and keeps water out. Since a C-1 is less stable than an open canoe, a good Eskimo roll is an essential and basic skill.

Though today's C-1 designs look much like kayaks, there are some fundamental differences. A kayaker sits with his legs in front of him and paddles with a double-bladed paddle; a C-1 paddler kneels, as in an open boat, and paddles with a single-bladed canoe paddle. A kayak has an oval or keyhole-shaped cockpit; that of a C-1 is round. The strokes that propel a C-1 are essentially the same as those described in this book. Thus it is often easier for an open-canoe paddler to move to a C-1 than to start over again in a kayak. C-1s are also somewhat easier to learn to roll.

Although there are some older C-1 designs (the Hahn, for example) that handle much like an open canoe, the tendency has definitely been toward lower-volume, race-inspired boats. Much of the design work in this field has been done by former U.S. and world champion Davey Hearn and friends. The Max series of boats (Max, Max II, UltraMax, CudaMax, and BatMax) have pretty much defined the racing C-1 world, and it's not unusual now to see these boats on the river as cruisers. They reward an expert's touch, but these boats aren't what one would consider to be user friendly. Hearn also designed a plastic cruising C-1, the GyraMax, a more forgiving design that has been a big hit with recreational paddlers.

Although the strokes may be the same, there are

Older large-volume C-1 designs, such as the Hahn, make the transition from open to decked canoe easier.

some big differences in handling between low-volume C-1s and open canoes. Modern C-1s, following the lead of the Max boats, have markedly asymmetric hulls that are designed to be steered more from the bow than from the stern. This allows the paddler to use positive forward strokes for maximum speed. To turn, for example, he would use a bow draw rather than a stern pry. The narrow bow also makes a forward stroke more effective by allowing the paddle to be brought closer to the boat's centerline. Because the boat is so small and light, the paddler can radically shift the pivot point forward or back, even to the point of sinking the stern underwater and rotating the boat around it. This pivot turn revolutionized slalom racing and led to the development of squirt boating.

If white water becomes your main interest, you'll probably want to try a C-1 at some point. For the ultimate in responsiveness, try a racing C-1. However, if you jump directly from an open boat to a low-volume C-1, you may become frustrated. To stick with something more predictable and familiar, a good choice for an easier transition is an older, high-volume C-1, of seventies vintage.

Flat Water

Based on some admittedly inexact statistics, there are about twice as many flatwater paddlers as whitewater paddlers. But (mutual put-downs aside) this division is getting less meaningful as more people paddle both types of water. *Flatwater* isn't an exact term, since it also includes a fair amount of paddling on the moving water of rivers. Sometimes it just refers to what the water rat calls "messing around in boats." You can have just as much fun thrashing around on a lake or floating down a sluggish river as on the biggest rapids. The distinctive variations of flatwater paddling all have their own boats, gear, gurus, and saints, as well as mental baggage. Let's quickly review some of the most important.

TRIPPING. The North Woods style of tripping and paddling is what springs into most people's minds when you say "canoe." As a sport and an art form it is still alive and well, and in some cases is practiced very much in the same manner as it was in the days of the voyageurs. Though the classic wood-and-canvas North

Tripping takes the canoe where it was meant to go—into the North Woods. (Photo: Jim Henry/Mad River Canoe)

Woods canoe is still in use, you can choose from more modern materials. The big difference today, however, is that tripping is done for enjoyment rather than for commercial reasons.

For an all-round experience including lakes and rivers, camping and portage, and wilderness exploration, this type of paddling is hard to beat. And the areas open to this type of travel are truly vast: the upper Northeast, the northern Midwest, and a great deal of Canada. The late Bill Mason immortalized this type of paddling and tripping in numerous films and books, so much so that I do not pretend to improve on what he has said or done (see the Resources section for a listing of Mason's work).

For most of us, alas, tripping from thaw to freeze-up will remain a vivid dream. We will have to keep paddling on weekends. If you are able to take the time and make the commitment to do this type of paddling, however, I recommend that you study the books specifically on the subject. If, on the other hand, you are more of a sports-oriented recreational paddler, you are advised to follow the path laid out between the pages of this book rather than of the voyageurs.

CRUISING AND FAST TOURING. One of the more distinctive flatwater schools is that of the fast cruisers. You shall know them by their boats, which are long, straight, and sleek, and also by the way they flash past you on the river. Their spokesman and chief advocate is Harry Roberts, formerly editor of the old (and greatly missed) *Wilderness Camping* magazine, and now editor of *Paddler* magazine.

Fast cruising boats look a bit like downriver boats. They are narrow, long, and inclined to be somewhat tippy. However, they are also fast and a real pleasure to paddle as long as you don't need to make any quick maneuvers. A good example of this type of boat is the Sawyer Summersong.

Harry has long been one of the chief advocates of the sit'n'switch school of paddling, which he calls the North American Touring Technique. This is an efficient, easy-to-learn method of paddling that lends itself well to bent-shaft paddles. It has recently been incorporated by the ACA into its canoe instruction program (see chapter 3 for a description).

If your paddling path takes you on slow rivers and lakes, and you enjoy slipping along downriver with the water burbling quickly alongside, give this type of paddling a try.

FREESTYLE. Freestylers are the nonconformists of the flatwater world. The concept sprang, Athene-like, from the mind of Mike Galt. Not only is Galt one of the chief practitioners of the art, he designs the state-of-the-art freestyle boats and writes long, mystic articles about the philosophy of freestyling. I don't know who names the moves in freestyling, but you may at first think you have entered an alien world when you hear talk of on-side static axles, reverse christies, and the like. But on second look you'll see that these are a restatement, rather than a reinvention, of paddling physics. This is not to say that the moves are easy. In fact, freestyle is one of the more difficult branches of the sport to master. Since the water does not move, all power and balance must come from the paddlers themselves.

The boats, though, are jewels, since the freestyling market is small enough that they must be handmade. Freestyling eschews the sheer speed of the cruisers for radical turns and boat leans. A typical freestyle boat, such as the Galt Egret, has a long but graciously rounded hull, and is designed to be laid over to the gunnels and spun in its own length. They are also great general-purpose fun boats, and very adept at things like picking their way through a Florida swamp. Whereas a cruiser requires room to breathe, a freestyle boat lets you have a lot of fun on very little water.

FLATWATER RACING. Most flatwater races are contests of speed and endurance rather than maneuverability. Marathon racing is very popular in the Midwest, with events that range from relatively short sprint events to multiday courses hundreds of miles long. Boats for these races are built for one thing: forward speed. Most pure racing designs have asymmetric Kevlar hulls, little freeboard, and lots of radical tumble home to get the paddles close to the boat's centerline. Typically the gunnels are pulled way in for the bow paddler. By touring standards, these boats are very unstable.

Speaking of marathons, one of the toughest races anywhere is the Texas Water Safari, 260 grueling miles over water ranging from mild white water to open bays. Snakes, alligators, and low-head dams add to the challenge. Finishing times vary with the water level, and winning times range from just over thirty-five hours in a wet year to fifty-four hours of nonstop, pain-fogged paddling in a dry one.

NINE

Boats and Equipment

NOT SO VERY LONG AGO, a canoe was a canoe. Canoes were all made of aluminum or wood and canvas, and had the traditional Hiawatha-style raised bow and stern. Racer Jamie McEwan remembers:

"A seventeen-foot, eighty-pound, shoe-keel Grumman canoe used to be not just the standard boat, but basically the only boat. It was whitewater and flatwater, singles and doubles, slalom and downriver. For big water, you taped on a canvas deck or bolted on plywood panels. The boat did everything, went everywhere. Because there was just one boat for all purposes, every*one* did everything, too. If there was a race, you raced. If there was a trip planned, you ran that river."

Today there are many canoes. Fast ones and slow ones, fat ones and skinny ones, short ones and long ones. Boats of all shapes, sizes, and materials. Which one is right for you? Making the right choice isn't always easy. As with most other things, it depends. Are you paddling primarily in white water, flat water, or a combination? Solo or tandem, or both? Is racing in the plan? How about family outings? The more technical aspects of canoe design can and do fill books, but before delving into this trove of knowledge, let's look at the hows and whys of some basic types of boats. Boat designers—and paddlers—start with a boat's intended function and go from there.

Canoe Design

All canoes have a *hull*, which may be made of materials ranging from wood and canvas to Kevlar or ABS. *Gunnels* of metal, wood, or plastic form the top of the boat's sides. (They were not, as we have seen, put there as handles.) *Thwarts* run across the inside of the boat. Both gunnels and thwarts stiffen the boat, as do optional *deck plates* at the bow and stern. The boat's *seats* also serve this purpose, in addition to providing a place to park the paddler's keester. Seats can be plastic, metal, wood and cane, or a foam or metal saddle.

Next, let's look at design characteristics. Notwithstanding what you will read in manufacturers' literature, there is no ideal canoe, though there may be one that's ideal for *you*. All boats, big and small, even general-purpose recreational canoes, are the result of design trade-offs. A general-purpose canoe might not do anything really well—or badly. At the other end

The parts of a canoe.

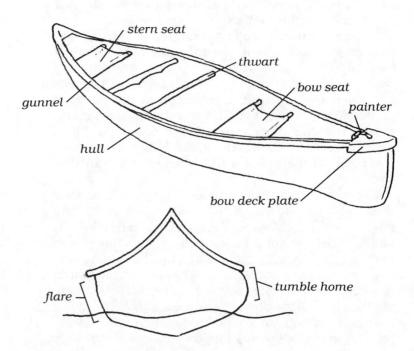

of the design spectrum are specialized designs like whitewater play boats and racing canoes, which do their intended job very well—and won't do anything else at all.

One of the most distinctive elements of any canoe's design is *rocker*, loosely defined as the amount of curve in a boat's hull from bow to stern, just as in a rocking chair. A boat with a straight keel from stem to stern has no rocker. Put it on a level surface and it sits flat from front to back. It resists turning, since the entire hull sits in the water with equal depth. But it is very easy to move in a straight line, since it resists the turning force of those unbalanced power strokes. The more rocker in the hull, the easier a boat is to turn, because the ends sit higher in the water and offer less resistance to sideways movement. The penalty is that movement in a straight line becomes harder, and every stroke tends to turn the boat. Some boats cleverly compromise by keeping a relatively straight keel for directional stability, then putting rocker on the *side* of the boat in a noticeable bulge. As long as the boat remains upright, it has little rocker. It goes straighter and faster. Lean it over, however, and the hull shape changes dramatically. The boat spins very fast on the bulge, often with the ends completely out of

Design characteristics of a canoe. Different features, like tumble home and flare, can be combined in a single hull (bottom right).

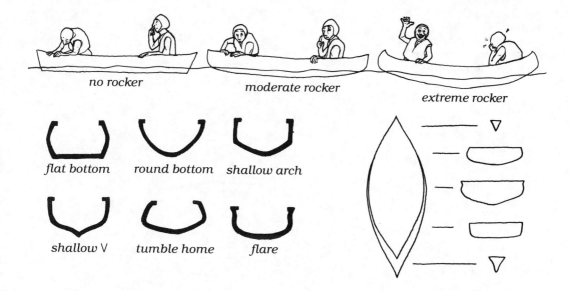

no rocker   moderate rocker   extreme rocker

flat bottom   round bottom   shallow arch

shallow V   tumble home   flare

the water. This, in effect, makes it a shorter boat with lots of rocker. Designers of flatwater freestyle boats and whitewater play boats both use this simple trick.

Generally, the longer a boat is in relation to its width, the faster it will be. A narrow boat also brings the paddler's forward stroke closer to the centerline of the boat, increasing its efficiency. Make a boat wider and it will be more stable. Make it narrower and it will go faster. Some boats are *symmetric*, which means that the bow and stern halves of the boat have the same shape, and some are *asymmetric*. Asymmetry usually improves speed: the designer can make the bow very sharp and finely tapered, so that the boat slices through the water.

The hull shape, as a cross section seen from the front of the boat, is a favorite topic of conversation among canoeists. The sides of a canoe may be *straight*, *flared* (curved away from the inside of the boat), or designed with *tumble home* (curved toward the inside of the boat). Bottoms are usually *flat*, *arched* (rounded), or *V-shaped*. The transition between hull and side is the *chine*. An abrupt transition is called a hard chine, and a smoother, more rounded one, a soft chine. The shape of a boat's chine usually

A canoe hull may be symmetrical (top), where the bow and stern have the same shape, or asymmetrical (bottom), where the bow is sharper than the stern.

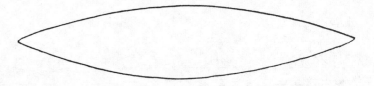

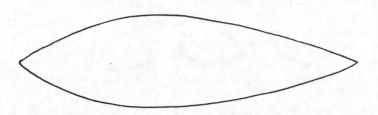

determines its manners when going from straight-up to laid over on its side.

Boats designed for big, windy lakes may have a *keel* running from bow to stern. A keel makes the boat track better and reduces side slipping. The advantage of a keel, however, is pretty much restricted to this specific situation, so unless your paddling is completely limited to lakes, you are better off without one.

The combination of these design factors defines the nature of a boat's performance. At one end of the scale is the ubiquitous aluminum johnboat. It has a flared hull, flat bottom, and *very* hard chine. As a result, it has a very high initial stability, but a well-deserved reputation for turning over without warning once the critical angle has been exceeded. On the other end of the spectrum are whitewater boats and freestyle flatwater boats, which have more rounded bottoms and much more subtle transitions from bottom to side. These boats *feel* more tippy initially, but since they are designed to be leaned to the gunnels in a turn, they have considerable *reserve*, or final stability. Make the hull too rounded, however, and there is often no stopping point once the boat starts to roll over—it just keeps right on going.

The bow and stern of the boat are usually described as *full* or *thin*, meaning that they are either blunt or pointed. A whitewater boat has full ends (and perhaps flared sides as well) to give the bow extra volume so that it can ride up over a wave that would otherwise bury it. A fast cruiser, on the other hand, has a very fine, thin bow (and probably an asymmetric hull) to knife through the water easily. Each works fine for its intended purpose, but an exchange can be frustrating. On white water, our tourer swiftly buries itself under the first wave, and ploughing a whitewater boat across a blustery lake is agony. Fullness is related to a boat's *depth*. A boat with more depth will run through bigger waves but at the cost of catching more wind.

Let's see how the designer and the paddler sort all this out.

FLATWATER CANOES. A flatwater boat may be intended for any one of several things. It might be a fast tourer, expected to put a lot of water under the hull in

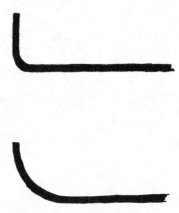

The chine is where the hull curves upward. A hard chine (top) means an abrupt transition, whereas a softer chine (bottom) has a smoother curve, easing the transition when leaning the boat over.

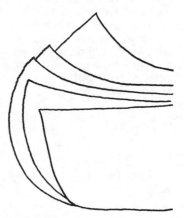

Canoe bows assume many shapes.

a minimum of time. In that case, the designer might make it long and narrow, with thin ends and an asymmetric hull. Rough-water stability isn't really a factor here, so the paddler would probably rather sit than kneel. The boat's keel will be straight from one end of the boat to the other, with little or no rocker. Since we don't expect to be crossing Lake Erie, the boat can be designed with less depth and a low, wind-cheating bow and stern. The resulting boat will be very fast when it moves in a straight line but unwilling to turn. This reluctance to turn allows the paddler to hustle along with the sit'n'switch technique of forward paddling, rather than using J-strokes or forward strokes with a correcting pry.

For a freestyle boat—to be used for playing and showing off, but not for extensive tripping or touring—the designer might select a short, low, symmetric hull with soft chines and a rounded bottom. The boat

Long, skinny, and fast—this Sawyer tourer shows off the design features of the breed. Note the long, sharp, asymmetric bow, radical tumble home, and low overall height. The paddler sits with his feet braced against an adjustable bar, and propels the boat with a bent shaft paddle.

A freestyle boat. With full ends and soft chines, this boat is made for turning and playing rather than for forward speed. It is stable even when leaned over to the gunnels.

might have some lift on the ends, but the keel would be relatively straight. There would, however, be a lot of curve on the sides of the hull. A kneeling paddler could then spin this boat in its own length by slamming it down to the gunnels. It's a fine design for small lakes, flatwater rivers, and swamps, although it will be much slower in a straight line than a slender tourer.

Single-purpose boats are great, but what about compromise? What you will often see marketed as a commodity item is the canoe equivalent of the johnboat. This general-recreation boat is generally around sixteen feet long, blunt-bowed, flat-bottomed, and *very* beamy. This satisfies those folks who just want to float down the river with a six-pack, or for whom the illusion of stability is paramount. There's certainly nothing wrong with this (go light on the six-pack, please), but if you're going to approach canoeing as a sport, you can do better.

A better overall compromise is the canoe developed in the Great North Woods not for recreation, but for the hard work of transporting people, supplies, and a winter's load of furs up and down rivers both flat and turbulent, across lakes, and over portages—all in the same canoe. This is a specialized type of paddling, but the boats that evolved there have long been accepted as the very definition of a canoe. They are mostly

Tripping boats, such as this Jensen-designed Wenona, have deep hulls to accommodate a load. (Photo: Wenona Canoe)

deep, flat-bottomed tandem boats, with high sides to repel both lake and whitewater waves. The ends are high, fuller than a flatwater cruiser but thinner than a pure whitewater boat, with no adornments like flare or tumble home. Most are seventeen to eighteen feet long, and paddlers may stand, sit, or kneel according to the situation.

WHITEWATER CANOES. After reading the preceding chapters, we would certainly conclude that one of the most desirable characteristics of a whitewater boat would be dryness. Ideally the boat should keep out most waves, but if we made the boat deep enough for heavy white water, the gunnels would be up to the paddler's armpits. We could flare the sides to deflect waves, but doing so would make the boat wider and reduce the efficiency of paddle strokes, especially for paddlers with short arms. Making only the bow and stern high, full, and flared does work, however, and this has become common practice.

The other important trait of a whitewater boat is the ability to change direction quickly. This requires a highly rockered hull. The boat is harder to paddle in a straight line, but this is a necessary trade-off, since little time in white water is spent going straight. The designer may, however, place more rocker on the side of the boat, so that the boat tracks under power while crossing a series of squirrelly crosscurrents, then turns easily when leaned over. The hull's cross section, on the other hand, is usually rounded, although some boats use V-shaped hulls. Surprisingly, a flat-bottomed hull works, too, since it draws less water. This gives much the same effect as rocker—a shallow draft offers less resistance to spinning the boat—while not making the boat so hard to keep straight. The disadvantage of a flat bottom, however, is the necessarily abrupt transition (hard chine) between the bottom and the side of the hull. This gives great initial stability but takes away reserve.

The ends of a whitewater canoe must be full enough to shed water and ride over waves. Make them too blunt, however, and the boat becomes a dog, unable to make crosscurrent moves.

The result is a witches' brew of compromise and concession that has occupied the hands and minds of Steve Scarborough, Nolan Whitesell, Eugene Jensen, and others. There are no easy answers, and each boat has a distinctive feel arising from its designer's pride and prejudices. We may be in a golden age of white-water canoe design, with new models appearing, it sometimes seems, almost daily. All of which makes it impossible to recommend specific boats in this book. But we won't leave you totally on your own. At the end of this section are some buyer's guidelines.

Materials

Design is only half the measure of a boat. The other half is the materials from which it is constructed. And whereas the design of modern canoes is in many respects very similar to that of canoes made hundreds or even thousands of years ago, the materials have changed considerably, allowing new shapes (wood only bends in certain ways), incredible strength, and a lightness never before known. As in boat design, there are different materials for different purposes.

ALUMINUM. When Grumman produced the first ninety-four aluminum canoes in 1945, the material had the glamor of being an aircraft material. Aluminum is very strong, reasonably light (seventy-five pounds for a seventeen-foot boat), and given proper care, will last several lifetimes. Writer Elliot Dubois still has a Grumman that he purchased in the late forties. This durability has endeared the "ironboat" to liveries, where you may still find them. Unfortunately, the design has not changed since aluminum's glory days. The white metal does not lend itself to exotic, slippery shapes, it is noisy and cold, and it tends to stick rather than slide on rocks. Wrap an aluminum canoe around a rock and you have sculpture, a disaster forever frozen in metal. A keel is part of the manufacturing process, and you can't get a boat without one. Thus, by today's standards, aluminum boats are really suited only for casual recreational use.

WOOD. In the world of canoeing, a wooden canoe means a *stripper*, that is, a boat made from thin strips of wood (cedar is a favorite) running from bow to stern. Strippers are lovely, expensive, and somewhat impractical boats that belong more to the world of fine art than to the day-to-day world of paddling. They are usually made on a custom basis. A properly constructed one is, however, nearly as strong as an aluminum boat.

WOOD AND CANVAS. Wood and canvas, often considered the traditional materials for a canoe, postdate birch bark but predate aluminum. They are still used every day for work and guide boats in the North Woods. Each of these boats starts as a wooden skeleton, over which is stretched a skin of canvas. The canvas is then sealed with varnish or paint. This type of construction, though not as strong as most others, is surprisingly durable. Since wood-and-canvas boats require a lot of hand work to construct, they are expensive, and offer little other than tradition and aesthetics to justify the extra cost. Wood-and-canvas canoes require periodic maintenance, and the canvas can soak up water, increasing the boat's weight. Wrap one and it becomes part of canoeing history. But if you are dead set against twentieth-century materials and don't plan on pushing the extremes, wood and canvas might be the thing for you.

FIBERGLASS. Fiberglass canoes were the next step after wood and canvas. Fiberglass is more malleable than almost any material in boat building. It is a plastic medium that has allowed designers a freedom never before dreamed of. Whatever shape their minds could devise could now be made to float. Make a mold, put the wet cloth in it, and wait for it to harden. *Voilà!* A new boat. Even though purists hated it (and still do), fiberglass took canoe design out of the doldrums and into new currents. It also affected the economy of boat building. Although the materials, at least initially, were as expensive as some others, a fiberglass boat could be built in much less time on a production-line basis, making for a lower-priced, more affordable boat.

Fiberglass boats come in two main varieties: chopper-gun and laid-up boats. The chopper gun uses compressed air to spray small particles of fiberglass into a mold saturated with hardener. The resulting boat, though very quick and inexpensive to manufacture, tends to be heavy and comparatively weak. Therefore, chopper-gun boats usually inhabit the lower end of the price-and-performance spectrum.

Other fiberglass boats use a layup: layers of fiberglass cloth (or cloth of any of a dozen other materials) are handlaid into the mold in layers. Eventually they harden into a single piece. This process makes it easy to reinforce different areas of the boat with extra layers of cloth. Laid-up construction is necessarily handwork, done with some extremely noxious materials—factors that drive up the cost.

By itself, fiberglass is not much lighter or stronger than wood, and is much more brittle. A 'glass boat will often shatter under a hard impact and is a definite write-off when wrapped. Yet fiberglass boats today still represent the mainstream of canoe design, offering shapes that no other material will assume.

PROPRIETARY LAYUPS. Given the shortcomings of fiberglass, it wasn't long before space-age materials like Kevlar, carbon fiber, and nylon found their way into the hands of inventive boat designers. These materials could be shaped like fiberglass but were stronger than steel. Another new world opened, with boats that were half the weight of their predecessors, but stronger. There was a price, of course—these new boats were two or three times as expensive as the old ones, which limited them to roles like racing, where light weight and strength were critical and cost was not. Most offered a mix of materials, balancing the factors of price, strength, and weight. Different properties could be combined—fiberglass could be laid on the outside to protect the Kevlar, which was strong but had poor abrasion resistance, and so forth, resulting in a laminated boat of many different materials.

Composite layup offers a flexibility in construction

equaled by no other procedure, but it is also one of the most costly. And finally, even space-age materials are not yet capable of beating the river in a one-on-one shoving match around a rock. Wrap a lovely, light-weight, expensive canoe of proprietary layup and you still have a wrapped canoe. It *may* be possible to salvage it, but not without a lot of work.

ABS AND OTHER PLASTIC. Finally, there is that other space-age material: plastic. The most common plastic used for canoe construction is ABS. This plastic (often marketed under trade names like Royalex and Ram-X) is actually a foam core sandwiched between two plastic sheets. ABS is a *thermoplastic*, molded under heat, and has the unique property of remembering its proper shape. This quality, combined with its natural toughness, makes it nearly ideal for the abusive world of whitewater canoeing. An ABS boat simply bounces off most obstacles and, unlike aluminum, does not stick on rocks. Small dings can be removed with a heat gun, and with a little help, even a wrapped boat resumes its shape after recovery—most of the time, anyway. ABS boats have been wrapped, thrown off the tops of buildings and speeding cars, and generally mistreated without permanent ill effect. It's no surprise that ABS virtually monopolizes whitewater.

But no material is perfect, and neither is ABS. For all its strength, ABS has a low resistance to abrasion. Whitewater boats often wear through the outer layer of plastic on the bow and stern. And although the technology is improving, ABS at present cannot be shaped with anywhere near the same freedom as fiberglass. It is also a relatively heavy material: an ABS canoe weighs about as much as one made from aluminum or wood and canvas. Because of its relative flexibility compared with fiberglass or composite materials, large ABS boats often suffer from "oilcanning" (the flexing of large areas of the hull under stress). For these reasons, fiberglass and composite boats still dominate the flatwater market.

One other recent development has been the production of canoes of rotomolded plastic. Until very recently, this method had been confined to making whitewater kayaks and decked canoes. In rotomolding, molten plastic is poured into a rotating mold to cool. Rotomolded boats have all the advantages of ABS, plus superior abrasion resistance and a range of shaping approaching that of fiberglass. The big disadvantage, however, has been lack of rigidity. Even in small rotomolded boats like kayaks, oilcanning is often a problem, and the boats must be extensively braced with internal walls. So far, this has limited plastic rotomolding to some small solo prototypes.

A Buyer's Mini-Guide

Buying a canoe can be an expensive proposition, and nobody wants to spend a lot of money for something that turns out to be wrong. Now that Jamie McEwan's old Grumman—the boat that did everything—is dead, the trend is toward multiple boats and specialized designs. You will do better to buy a boat suited for the type of paddling you do most, and not try to find a canoe that will do a little bit of everything.

A temptation at the outset is often to buy some ragged-out piece of junk. I can get it cheap, so the thinking goes, and therefore if I decide I don't like it, or don't like canoeing, I won't have that much tied up in it. Usually, this is a mistake. You may end up with something so totally unsuitable that you'll sour on the sport without having really given it a chance. Suppose you buy some nice, stable barge. It won't turn over, sure, but by the end of the day, after having tried in vain to keep up with your friends, you're whipped and thinking that canoeing is not for you. But it was cheap, right?

The other extreme is to buy a hot boat right away. This might be a racer, a smoking pistol of a freestyle boat, or the very latest whitewater wonder. The theory here is that since you'll never outgrow the boat, you'll have saved yourself the cost of a beginner boat. And it does look cool on top of your car. All true, but you may never learn to paddle it at all. You may instead spend many frustrating hours going in circles or investigating the bottoms of rivers and ponds, only to conclude that snorkeling might be your sport of choice after all.

There are better, less frustrating ways. Read magazines. *Canoe* magazine's buyer's guide is particularly good, as is their annual "Starting Out" issue. *Paddler* magazine, which incorporated *Canoesport Journal* and *River Runner*, covers both flat and white water. These magazines test and review boats, as well as offer frequent articles on technique.

Take a clinic. This is one of the best ways to get your feet wet in the sport. It might be a whitewater clinic from a large and internationally known organization, like the Nantahala Outdoor Center, or an informal clinic given by the local canoe shop for prospective customers. This is a good chance to try different boats before you buy. What do canoe clinics in your area use for instruction? This is usually a good indicator of what works for beginners (although, in fairness, they might be there because the organization is a dealer). Any good clinic boat should be a compromise between good performance and a forgiving nature.

Join a canoe club. The favorite topic of conversation is usually boats. Clubs often have their own instructional systems, and people are usually happy to let you try their boats. They may even steer you to a good used boat. Talk to people about boats, but be warned, paddlers tend to be a *very* opinionated lot and sometimes try, retrospectively to justify a boat just purchased. Pick the one *you* like.

Another consideration is resale value. You may, in time, decide to move on to that spiffy high-tech Kevlar wonder. If so, you will find that it is much easier to sell a popular boat than that old barge you bought.

Should it be tandem or solo? Don't automatically go tandem because you're a couple. Tandem canoes, instead of being love boats, can be divorce makers. ("Dammit, I *said* right!") Many couples, in the interest of harmonious relations, are switching to solo boats. Some canoes, such as the Dagger Caper, can be set up either tandem or solo. However, a boat much over fifteen feet can be a handful for a single paddler.

Outfitting

After buying a boat but before paddling it, you'll need to *outfit* it. For some flatwater boats, this means little more than tying in a water bottle. For most whitewater boats, however, the process can be quite extensive and time-consuming. What you want is a boat that fits *you* and is set up to allow you to paddle it the way you want. Sometimes, this isn't as easy as it sounds. An alternative to the process outlined below is to let some-

one else do it. Some outfitter's shops, like the Nantahala Outdoor Center Outfitter's Store, offer a custom
boat-outfitting service on a per-hour basis. Another
example is Whitesell Canoe, which virtually insists on
selling you a custom-outfitted boat.

There are two basic concepts that underlie outfitting. One is getting the trim, or weight bias of the boat,
correct. Since we want the boat's trim to be neutral or,
in a solo boat, slightly sternward, we have to sit or
kneel in the right place. For a solo boat the process is
simple: have a friend watch while you slide back and
forth just offshore. With a tandem boat, the paddlers
are often different sizes and weights. Some flatwater
boats, especially those designed for sit'n'switch paddling, have sliding seats, which makes trimming very

*The tools of the trade for
flatwater: adjustable sliding
seat, foot brace, and bent
shaft paddle.*

simple. You can even adjust the trim while under way. Otherwise, you will have to move the seat (or install a new one) to get the correct trim—often a laborious process.

The other basic outfitting concept is that no matter what the boat's use, the paddler needs a way to fuse himself to the boat so that when he plants the paddle (in concrete, right?) and pulls, *all* the power from the stroke is transferred to the boat. If the paddler's body, specifically either his knees or fanny, slides around, a sizable amount of that power is wasted. Better flat-water boats have seats shaped like tractor seats, which work very well to keep one's butt in place. Otherwise, it's a good idea to tape or glue some foam blocks on the seat to keep you from sliding around. Racers do this as a matter of course. If you're sitting, not only your be-hind but your feet need a positive stop as well. Some boats have adjustable foot bars in front of the seats, and putting your feet on these and pushing against the seat can really lock you in for effective stroking. If your flatwater boat doesn't have a foot bar, you might consider adding one, even if it's no more than a dowel or a block of foam glued to the bottom of the boat.

The kneeling position of the whitewater paddler allows a lower center of gravity and a three-point con-tact between paddler and boat, but the principle of locking yourself in is the same. However, you must compromise the outfitting enough so that you can get out when you need to. The paddler kneels on cupped pieces of foam (which keep his knees from sliding) and uses *thigh straps* to keep himself fastened to the boat. These straps are usually anchored between the paddler's knees and extend over his thighs, each to another anchor point near one of the gunnels. The straps should come over the lower part of the thighs and not fit so far up that it is difficult to slide out of them in an emergency. If you do install thigh straps (or buy a boat with them installed), make sure that there is a quick release on *both* straps in case something goes wrong.

Some paddlers also install *toe blocks* so that they can push themselves into the thigh straps, even when upside-down. These are indispensable if you are plan-ning to do Eskimo rolls.

Outfitting for whitewater boats tends to be more complex. There are a variety of saddles, pedestals, and thwarts to choose from. The saddle installed in this boat is made for two paddlers. Thigh straps and air bags are also considered mandatory in most places.

If you're in a tripping boat and do not anticipate severe white water, it may be enough to switch from a sitting to a kneeling position when the need arises by simply sliding your feet underneath the seat and dropping to your knees on a glued-in foam slab.

Many paddlers prefer to sit on thwart seats, feeling that these give them better control. If the paddler attaches a block to the thwart on either side of his butt to keep it from sliding around, any force from his body will instantly be transferred via the thwart to the gunnel and to the hull. Depending on the boat, however, it's sometimes hard to get a thwart at exactly the right height and place. Thwarts are also narrow and hard to sit on for extended periods of time.

Some other alternatives for sitting are a *saddle* of foam, plastic, or metal, or a foam *pedestal* seat. These are usually held in position by the thwarts. The metal saddles are adjustable; foam saddles and pedestals can be cut to fit. Several designs have integral foot braces and attachment points for thigh straps, which simplifies the job of outfitting.

TRIM. While you're outfitting, take a look at the trim. Here we mean thwarts and gunnels, not the balance of the boat. In fact, take a look at them before you

Terry Hill's custom "erector set" saddle offers nearly infinite adjustability. The seat slides back and forth on a track and can also be moved up and down.

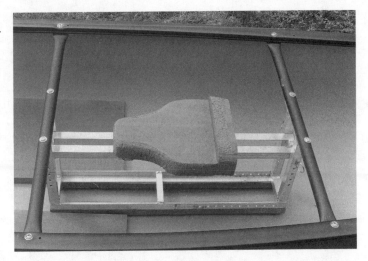

buy the boat. Thwarts and gunnels are usually made from wood, plastic, or metal and add strength and rigidity to any boat. For additional strength, some boats also have metal deck plates at the apex of the gunnels at bow and stern. Wooden trim is beautiful (oiled mahogany is particularly elegant) but not as strong as ugly metal. Wood is fine for flat water but can be downright dangerous on white water. If a wood-trimmed boat gets wrapped or sometimes even roundly thrashed in a hole, the trim can break into spears of shattered wood. Wrap a boat with metal trim and you can generally beat it back into place: wooden thwarts and gunnels will have to be replaced. Metal gunnels do have the disadvantage of picking up burrs on which you can cut yourself. It's a good idea to go over the boat periodically with a file to remove them.

PAINTERS. To make handling easier most boats have *painters*, or lines, attached to bow and stern. These can be a great help in tying the boat down or in rescue. A good rule of thumb is to keep your painters in the six- to ten-foot range. Polypropylene rope, preferably a bright color so that you can see it, is best. Nylon sinks in the water and Manila isn't strong enough. When you're paddling, painters should be stowed so that they don't trail in the water, yet you must be able to reach them if you need to swim the boat over to shore after a spill. There are various solutions to this problem, ranging from stuffing each painter under an air bag to tucking it neatly beneath an elastic draw cord on the deck plate. It's a good idea, especially on white water, to stow everything in the boat and avoid trailing any lines or gear that might entangle a swimmer.

FLOTATION. Any canoe needs some kind of flotation, either included in the design of the boat or added during the outfitting process. The only question is how much. Even in the flattest of waters, a boat with no flotation will sink, making for an embarrassing situation. Even flatwater boats usually have some type of built-in flotation—an air chamber or a small block of foam glassed into the bow and stern under the deck plates. Though this keeps the boat from disappearing on a lake, it may not be enough to keep your boat from submarining elsewhere. The higher the boat rides in the water after it has capsized, the easier it is to recover. This is true whether you have to swim it out of a whitewater river or tow it to shore across a windy lake.

In white water, flotation is vital for two reasons: first, flotation excludes water, making the boat less prone to swamping, as well as lighter and marginally more manageable even when full of water. Second, since the boat floats higher, it is less prone to wrap around obstacles like rocks. For these reasons you see many whitewater boats stuffed absolutely full of flotation, leaving barely enough room for the paddler. Nolan Whitesell, who's paddled runs like Niagara Gorge, advises leaving enough room in front of the paddler to bail with the paddle (read about the roll in chapter 7).

Another complication is that the more flotation you add, the less room there is for gear—a serious consideration for multiday wilderness trippers. You can add some extra flotation by lacing planks of two-inch Ethafoam along the sides of the boat (a method long favored by the Coastal Canoeists). This is acceptable for moderate white water and still leaves room for a goodly amount of duffel. Another solution is to place all gear in waterproof bags, and then tie these in as if they were air bags. If the canoe is very heavily loaded, however, it may be almost as difficult to manage as if it were full of water. Some trippers prefer to tie duffel in so as to be able to release it quickly (with a line to keep it near the canoe), then flip the boat upright (see the Capistrano Flip in chapter 10) and reel the duffel back in.

Right now the overall best solution for white water is to use air bags for flotation. For a solo boat this means bow and stern bags, and for tandem boats, a large center bag and perhaps small bow and stern bags. Air bags have to be firmly anchored to be effective. It's no good if the bags float to the surface and leave the boat underwater. Many whitewater paddlers stretch a network of nylon cord above the bag to keep it in place, in addition to mooring it firmly to the hull.

Some outfitters have used foam blocks wedged under the thwarts in the center of the canoe to provide both flotation and, in case of a pin, rigidity (something that air bags don't provide). These work well but take up a lot of room. And if made of Styrofoam (which they usually are because of cost), the blocks begin to deteriorate in a year or so, leaving an unsightly trail of debris on the river.

Paddles

The man on the other end of the stick was Harry Roberts, who has been paddling longer than most of us have been walking. "Let me see that thing, Harry," I said. It was a strange implement with a curved shaft and bent blade, made with woods of diverse character glued together, shaped and polished into a paragon of lightness and strength. It did not look like any paddle I had ever seen before. "What's the theory here?" I asked, fully expecting the type of lengthy technical explanation only a flatwater paddler can give. Harry just looked at me, puffed on his pipe a moment in the warm Maine afternoon, and said, "I like the way it feels." That, in the last analysis, is what paddle selection is all about.

The parts of a paddle.

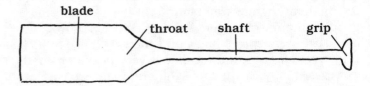

Next to boats, paddles probably account for the most arguments and six-pack conversations among canoeists. Maybe it's because unlike boat design (tekkies, forgive me), paddle design soars much higher into the ozone of subjectivity than many would like to admit. Some of the best whitewater paddlers I know, for example, customarily use a Carlisle, which is about as basic as paddles come. It has a hard thermoplastic blade, a vinyl-covered aluminum shaft, and a plastic T-grip. It looks and feels like a commodity item rather than the artful interface of man and canoe. It is definitely not a blade for purists, but there's no question that it works.

Nevertheless, there are a few guideposts along the way through the touchy-feely world of paddle selection. Let's go back to that Carlisle for a moment. Everything we've said so far about paddling suggests that the blade should be rigid. If the blade flexes, it wastes some of the power that we're trying to transfer to the boat. It's just like fitting yourself tightly in the boat: the less opportunity there is for power to leak out, the more that's left for propelling the boat. You can test this in the store by holding the T-grip of the paddle in one hand and putting the blade on the floor. Now push in the middle of the shaft with your other hand. If the blade gives, you can do better. Our Carlisle, for example, has a rigid (if somewhat unaesthetic) blade.

SHAFTS. A certain amount of give in the shaft, on the other hand, can work to your advantage. A *slight* springiness, such as that found in any wood paddle, acts as a shock absorber. This wastes a small amount of power, to be sure, but is much easier on your joints after a long day with a loaded canoe. Racers, who like to keep everything as rigid as possible, tend more toward synthetic paddles reinforced with the same kinds of space-age exotics as boats. I have, however, seen some big-name paddlers use paddles with rigid synthetic blades and wooden shafts, which proves that there is a place for everything. Some people, including myself, prefer the feel of a wooden paddle to that of a synthetic one, especially on cold days.

GRIPS. Those paddlers who do a lot of turning—whitewater paddlers, freestyle flatwater paddlers, and

Paddle blades and grips have many different shapes.

THE NORTH WOODS PADDLE
Probably the most idiosyncratic paddle concept is that of the North Woods tripping paddle, which has three shallow, scooped-out *stations* on the shaft. These paddles are very long with a thin, beavertail blade. (This is probably where the old "rule" about having a paddle that reaches to your chin came from.) The technique to be used with a paddle like this is very different from any we've described so far. Instead of using body rotation, the paddler uses the North Woods tripping stroke, pushing on the paddle station with his hand upside down (that is, with the thumb rotated down and the heel of the hand on the paddle station). He moves the paddle in an almost circular motion, keeping his shaft hand relatively fixed and pushing with his grip hand during the power phase. The blade seldom leaves the water, and is feathered during the recovery. Though this contradicts much of what we've said about paddling so far, it works well in the application for which it was intended: moving a loaded canoe along hour after hour. Once a heavy canoe like this gets up to cruising speed, it takes much less power to keep it there.

Why three stations? One for standing, one for sitting, and the bottom one for kneeling.

racers—prefer paddles with T-grips. The T-grip is exactly parallel to the paddle blade, giving instant feedback on the blade angle. Other paddlers, who move mostly in a straight line—trippers, marathon racers, and fast cruisers—often prefer a rounded knob as a grip.

BLADES. A great deal of pseudo-scientific nonsense has been published about the action of paddle blades in the water, as well as impassioned defenses and condemnations of various shapes. Most of these operate on the assumption that the *blade* moves through the water. Our assumption at the outset, you will recall, is that the blade does not move. The *boat* moves. Further, we know that most of a stroke's power is delivered during the first few inches of travel. What is important, then, is that the blade be rigid and that it have enough surface area to hold it in place long enough for the paddler to pull the boat forward.

Water, as we saw in chapter 1, does not compress. This gives it a unique property: pull or push on it suddenly and hard, as with a forward stroke or brace, and it acts almost as if it were solid. If you've ever fallen off a water ski at speed, you know what I mean. It is this phenomenon that holds the blade in place. Pull gently, however, and the water has more time to displace, flowing around the paddle and allowing it to slip through the water. Hence the earlier recommendation that you "explode" on the initial pull.

Blade area and shape are significant, but bigger is not necessarily better. A blade of enormous proportions might in theory waste little power, but it would be impossible to use. How big is enough? I can't tell you exactly, but it's significant that many paddlers have been downsizing their blades in recent years. You can add blade area to a paddle in two ways, by making the blade either wider or longer. Which you do is governed by the type of water you normally paddle. Paddles made for deep, unobstructed water (big lakes, rivers, and the ocean) tend to have long, narrow blades, usually in a *beavertail* or *tulip* shape. Paddles for shallow, rocky water are usually wider and more rectangular. Make the paddle too long and it becomes unwieldy and difficult to recover; make it too wide and it will hit the hull, interfering with your strokes.

Which brings us right back to our starting point: how does it feel?

BENT-SHAFT PADDLES. One other paddle variation, the bent shaft, is worth mentioning. Bent-shaft paddles were developed by flatwater marathon racers and have since been accepted for touring. The paddle shaft is bent at the throat, just above the blade, at an angle of 5 to 15 degrees. This type of paddle works best when used from a sitting position. As the boat moves forward toward the place where the paddle is planted, the bent shaft allows the paddle blade to stay nearly vertical longer. Flatwater sit'n'switch types,

Bent and straight sticks.

who do not use as much body rotation as the rest of us, swear by them. Though bent-shaft paddles are highly efficient for fast touring, they are less desirable for applications requiring frequent turns.

CONSTRUCTION AND DURABILITY. Of all the paddles we've discussed so far, only one is useless—the one that breaks. Durability is not necessarily related to price, since even cheap paddles can be quite durable. More so than with canoe design, however, paddle making quickly approaches the art and price tags of sculpture. But for someone who appreciates the finer things in life, a custom paddle is just the thing.

Paddles can be divided into two major categories: synthetic and wood. A few, however, have wooden shafts and synthetic blades. Synthetic paddles are made in a wide variety of constructions, from jerk-water basic to the wild voodoo sticks of the water gurus. Wooden paddles, on the other hand, are either carved from one piece of wood (the traditional beaver-tail is made this way) or are laminated from strips and pieces of wood glued together, much as a canoe is laid up. Laminated construction produces a stronger paddle and gives the paddle designer more freedom. Like makers of a proprietary layup boat, paddle makers mix different woods with diverse properties in the constant search for the lightest, strongest stick. Wooden paddles, though not as strong as synthetics, hold up surprisingly well, even under the unremitting abuse of white water.

Cost is always a big consideration, so test any paddle before you buy it. First, push on the shaft and blade as described earlier. The blade should be rigid and the shaft reasonably so. Then paddle with it. Where are you going to use it? Whitewater paddles are heavily reinforced; flatwater touring paddles can be made with a lighter construction. No one likes paddling with a war club, and frequently lightness, strength, and price are directly related. If you plan to paddle on shallow, rocky rivers, check the tips and edges of your prospective purchase, for this is where the river will chew at it. A wooden paddle intended for white water should be both *edged* (with a strip of harder wood, like hickory, glued to the outside of the blade) and *tipped* (with a tip of metal, hardwood, or some synthetic material inserted into or over the tip). Of these two modifications, the tip is the more important, but both will pay big dividends in durability.

And finally, there is a place for cheap paddles—everyone needs a spare.

Personal Gear

After thinking about the boat and the paddle, think of yourself. As for any other sport, certain items will make you safer, more comfortable, and lately, more stylish. Safety comes first.

FLOTATION AIDS. One item you should never be without (it is required by law in most places) is a life jacket or flotation aid. (You will also hear it referred to by its Coast Guard appellation, the personal flotation device or PFD. I personally prefer the German term *Schwimmweste*, or swimvest, which gives a better idea of what you're expected to do in one.)

Next to your boat, your life jacket will be one of the most important purchases you make, but it's almost easier to make the wrong choice than the right one. Though the primary purpose of a life jacket is simple—to hold your head above water so that you can breathe—there are several other significant things to consider as well.

To many, the most important thing about a life jacket is the amount of flotation. A more important question really is, how does it *fit*? You're going to be wearing this thing a lot, so make sure you like it. If your life jacket isn't comfortable, you may be tempted not to wear it. If it interferes with your paddling, it may lead to chafed arms or a missed move in white water. If the life jacket rides up while you're in the water and you cannot swim, you may be worse off than if you weren't even wearing one. It should fit your body closely and have a sturdy waist tie that locks with a positive device like a buckle. The rule here is that the life jacket must let you do what you need to do in the boat, and not hinder swimming if you're out of the boat. Talk with people who do your kind of paddling and see what they recommend.

Flotation is the next thing to think about. How far will you have to swim to safety, and through what kind of water? If you paddle on small lakes and small rivers, calm or whitewater, where the swim to shore is short, you may use a small jacket with fifteen to eighteen pounds of flotation. On big lakes, at sea, and on large, turbulent rivers, more flotation—up to twenty-five pounds—is needed. For offshore or big-lake rescue, especially if there is a chance of an extended wait in the water, thirty-five pounds is more appropriate. Big-lake paddlers face a problem here, since a vest this size is usually too bulky for comfortable paddling. So other factors come into play: your body type (skinny people need more flotation), and whether you'll be wearing a wetsuit or drysuit (either can provide an extra eight to ten pounds of flotation). You should also consider how good a swimmer you are and how comfortable you are in the water. In general, beginners should select bigger life jackets.

I have so far omitted the customary recitation of the Coast Guard PFD categories, but a brief look may be worthwhile, if only so that you'll know as much as the salesman.

*Type I*s are the original lifejackets with the full thirty-five pounds of flotation. They are just the thing if the *Love Boat* goes down and you are waiting in frigid waters for the Coast Guard cutter to arrive. Most of the flotation is in the front so that you'll float faceup even if you're unconscious (and if the water is calm). You will probably find these PFDs bulky and uncomfortable, although they are worth considering if you plan to paddle across Lake Superior.

*Type II*s—horse-collar life jackets—are better ignored. You can do better.

*Type III*s are the vest-type jackets most paddlers will wear, since they are made for active paddling (and swimming) rather than passive floating. Recently the Coast Guard has prohibited manufacturers from calling Type IIIs life jackets and has insisted that they be termed flotation aids instead.

*Type IV*s are throwable flotation devices, like ring buoys and boat cushions. Not primary life-support devices, they can be handy to throw to others in a pinch.

*Type V*s are anything else, including life jackets for commercial whitewater rafting, windsurfing, and the like. You may find something in this mixed bag that fits your needs, but make sure it is designed for boating (whitewater models are best) and not for another sport.

One other thing. Use your informed judgment to choose the best life jacket for you, and don't rely solely on the fact that the jacket you're looking at has the magic Coast Guard sticker. To be approved, a life jacket must only pass testing in a pool. Some places require a USCG-approved life jacket, and some do not. Check your state and local boating laws.

So far we've talked about considerations for first-time buyers. But what about those who already have life jackets? When is it time to buy another one? After all, age and sunlight will eventually kill any life jacket. Look it over for signs of deterioration, then put it on and give it the following test: jump into the water holding it in place. If your nose is underwater, it's time for a new life jacket. Now jump in again and release your hold on the jacket. If it floats up in front of your face, you need either to buy a new life jacket or to fix the waist ties.

A properly fitted life jacket is a must for any boater, no matter what the water. Make sure you have the right one for the paddling you do. Like any other form of insurance, if you need it and haven't got it, it's too late.

HELMETS. Most canoeists, even on white water, don't need a helmet. The exceptions are those who paddle Class III water or above, and paddlers who can do an Eskimo roll. If you get a helmet, buy a good sturdy one that doesn't slide around on your head, and *wear* it.

RIVER CLOTHING. There are three reasons for river clothing: style, utility, and safety. I cannot help you with style. The utility of items like hats, sunglasses, and the like is fairly obvious, but it's worth taking some time to consider the safety aspects of river clothing.

To survive on the river, we must keep our body temperature within fairly narrow limits. If it gets much under normal, we become hypothermic. We'll take a closer look at hypothermia in the next chapter, but for now let's just talk about keeping warm. You may be sweating while paddling, then suddenly get dunked into icy water. On lakes and rivers (especially at high altitude), weather conditions may change dramatically in a matter of minutes, and *any* canoeist risks getting soaked in a passing shower. All of which can cool you off in a hurry.

Your clothing can help keep you relatively comfortable at times like this. Avoid cotton clothing, which absorbs moisture and holds it next to your skin, giving you a cold, clammy feeling. It also takes a long time to dry, even on a warm day. Thus, jeans and T-shirts are out, except for the very warmest conditions (both air and water). Wool and synthetic pile garments are much more suitable. Wool and pile fibers do not absorb water, do dry quickly, and keep you warm even when wet.

Next consider the effect of wind chill. A stiff breeze can drop the effective temperature thirty or forty degrees in minutes, even on a warm day. In such conditions you need a windproof layer over the pile to keep out the wind. Nylon works well, either uncoated, if you expect not to get wet, or coated with a waterproof material, if you do. Whitewater paddlers customarily wear a *paddling jacket* of coated nylon that seals out waves, wind, and spray.

What we have just described is the layering system familiar to backpackers and most outdoors people. It works just as well on the river. As long as they do not hinder movement, several thin layers work better than one thick one and are more easily adjusted to changing conditions.

The type of clothes you wear is important, too. Make sure you can swim in them. Street clothes are difficult to swim in, as are entangling pieces of clothing like ponchos.

TIP: A piece of survival gear any paddler can carry is a small waterproof bag (a garbage bag will do) with an old wool sweater and a wind shell. Kept dry, these can be a real morale builder in an emergency.

If you paddle in cold weather, open water, extreme or expedition conditions, or on white water, you should consider wearing a wetsuit or drysuit. This is especially true if you're over forty. Open-weave garments of wool or pile are effective only *after* you get out of the water. While you're in it, water flows through the pile and conducts heat away from your body at an accelerated rate. Only a wetsuit or drysuit keeps you warm while *in* the water.

The wetsuit is made of neoprene and is designed to fit the body tightly. A small amount of water enters the space between the wearer's skin and the neoprene, acting as an additional insulating layer. It comes in various thicknesses for different conditions. Lighter wetsuits (made for surfing or boardsailing) are less confining and lend themselves better to layering. Wetsuits can be smelly and uncomfortable, but excel in extreme conditions.

A drysuit is, as the name implies, meant to keep you dry even in the water. The drysuit usually comes as either a one- or a two-piece outfit, or a dry top. It is usually constructed of coated fabric and sealed at the wrists, throat, and ankles by elastic latex seals. The drysuit fits loosely, and the paddler wears normal insulating pile clothing underneath. No drysuit is totally dry—all leak a bit at the seals. However, they are much more comfortable than wetsuits and very effective at conserving body heat. In warm weather, in fact, they can be too effective, and overheating becomes a problem. In addition, drysuits are also expensive, somewhat more delicate than wetsuits (the thin latex seals can tear and the waterproof zippers stick), and offer less physical protection from bumps when in the water.

FOOTWEAR. Feet often get overlooked in the outfitting process. An old pair of tennies will work, but there are alternatives. Sandals, for example, let water drain away from your feet in hot weather. In cold weather you'll want wetsuit booties of neoprene to keep your feet warm. If you anticipate a lot of scouting or lining, try the ones with the felt soles. They give much more secure footing on slippery rocks.

GLOVES. Your hands may need protection, too. If you have an office job and don't paddle much, a pair of paddling gloves will reduce the incidence of blisters. In cold, windy weather, hand protection is a must. Paddlers most often protect their hands with gloves or *pogies*, a hand cover made from fabric or neoprene that fits on the paddle shaft. If it's not too windy, a pogie on just the bottom hand may suffice. Neoprene or synthetic gloves also work well, but many paddlers find these confining.

Safety Gear

The safety gear needed on the vast majority of canoe trips is minimal. First and foremost is the paddling skill that allows you to avoid emergencies in the first place. Second is the knowledge of how to use safety and rescue gear. There is no piece of gear, however well designed, that cannot be misused, even to the extent of putting a victim in a worse situation than if it had not been used. Part of your education as a paddler is to learn basic safety and rescue procedures. We'll cover the particulars in a later chapter. For now, let's look at some common safety and rescue items. (For more details, see *River Rescue*.)

THROW BAGS. The throw bag is a fabric sack (usually nylon) into which is stuffed fifty to seventy feet of polypropylene rope. A chunk of foam inside makes it float. The most common task for throw bags is to retrieve swimmers and boaters on rivers. Whitewater paddlers should consider a throw bag (and learning to be proficient with it) as essential a part of their kit as the paddle. Flatwater paddlers have less need of a rope, but a throw bag is still a handy way to carry one. Ropes have many uses in shuttles, in camp, and on the river.

KNIVES. Anyone who works around ropes on the river should carry a knife. Entanglement of the victim or rescuer is always a possibility, and a quick slash from a sharp knife will free him. River knives should be of nonrusting stainless steel. Many paddlers prefer to carry them on their life jackets, where they are instantly available. Ideally, you should be able to operate your knife with one hand, even in less than perfect conditions.

WHISTLES. It's often hard to get someone's attention over the roar of the river. A good whistle will do it, as well as serving as a signaling device on the water.

SIGNALS. Paddlers on big lakes and in remote areas might want to consider other signal devices, such as smoke and small pen flares. A signal mirror works well for attracting the attention of aircraft.

CARABINERS. Carabiners perform a multitude of tasks on the river, from clipping in loose gear to substituting for a pulley in a mechanical haul system. They are cheap, require little maintenance other than occasional lubrication, and are easily carried. They are natural partners for the throw bag.

FIRST-AID KIT. The contents of your first-aid kit should increase in direct proportion to the distance from a hospital. For day trips close to a road, a simple "ouch pouch" with Band-Aids is plenty. If you anticipate a lengthy evacuation or extended care, plan accordingly. And remember, the best medical equipment is little good without the knowledge of how to use it.

EMERGENCY KIT. Sometimes things go wrong on the river. You may wrap or pin a boat and have to spend the night in an unexpected place. Or you may be overtaken by a storm that brings freezing rain and keeps you from paddling. A member of your party may get lost or injured. All these situations can be dealt with—if you are prepared. We have already mentioned keeping a bag with extra dry clothing even on a short trip. An even better idea, especially on a spring or fall trip, is to add a few emergency items: fire-starting materials like waterproof matches, a candle, or "fire ribbon"; a space blanket; and perhaps a small tube tent. These items weigh little and can be lifesavers.

TEN

Safety and Emergencies

CANOEING, even on white water, is a very safe sport—as long as you're willing to follow a few simple rules. Two groups are involved in most river accidents. First are the turkeys: people with little or no skill, experience, or knowledge of the river who get themselves into trouble through simple ignorance of the basic dangers of any body of water. They are the ones who blithely paddle over low-head dams or invite hypothermia by wearing cotton clothing on a cold, windy day. It's not unusual to see willful ignorance, either: someone who thinks that a couple of shots of John Courage will increase his chances of successfully running a certain rapid. The cure for this group is simple: a little river education and some common sense.

Having done this, the turkey now metamorphoses into a legitimate beginner. What's the difference? Attitude, mainly. The beginner knows he's got a lot to learn and the turkey thinks he already knows it all. The good news is that a lot of us who started canoeing with feathers have graduated into the safest paddlers on the river—beginner through advanced.

Not so long ago we could say that once you got past the turkey stage you were pretty safe. Lately, experts have taken to paddling water that allows little or no

*(Illustration by
William Nealy,
courtesy of Menasha
Ridge Press.)*

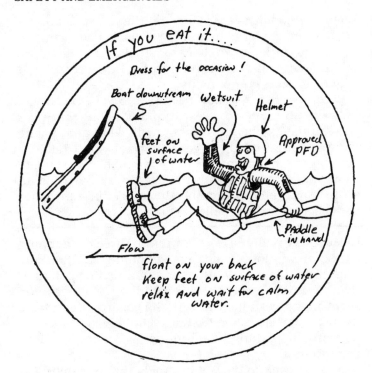

room for error, and their casualties have risen accordingly. Similarly, it used to be that open canoes never ventured into Class IV water. No longer. Open canoes have taken to water once reserved for decked boats, even to runs like Niagara Gorge. Readers of this book probably won't ever run water like this (neither has your author), but it's worth mentioning because just about everybody goes through what the American Canoe Association's safety chairman, Charlie Walbridge, calls "the crazy stage" in the progression from beginner to expert.

This stage is on the whole readily identified: the look in the paddler's eyes changes from terror or respect to one of crazed enthusiasm, and his conversation shifts from discussions of boat designs and paddling technique to constant name-dropping about the rivers he's run (or swum). Our timid beginner has become overconfident. Safety is now a joke, something for turkeys to worry about. Unfortunately, the only known cure for this stage is time. Sometimes this time is compressed when the paddler "sees God" on the river (usually at the bottom of a large hydraulic) or has a bad swim. Or it may go on for several seasons before he wises up. Fortunately, this stage is rarely fatal, however trying it may be to one's companions.

Naturally, this will never happen to you. But if you do wake up in a cold sweat thinking about that river you ran the day before, ask yourself: what am I trying to prove? Am I trying to get better at a sport I enjoy? Looking for the ultimate adrenaline rush? Or trying to show that I can run with the Big Dogs? Safety is an attitude as much as anything. It starts (and sometimes ends) between the paddler's ears.

River Hazards

River safety really breaks down into three overlapping parts: prevention, paddling technique, and rescue. Prevention means identification of a real or potential river hazard. Technique, or paddling skill, lets us avoid or successfully deal with the hazard. If that fails, the next step is rescue. Rescue technique is just as important as paddling technique, if somewhat less glamorous.

Let's go back to our set of rapids that our mythical paddler ran successfully in a previous chapter. Let's see if he can do it again. There he goes. This time, he misjudges the current slightly and instead of heading straight down through the waves, he hits them angled a bit too far to the left. The waves push the bow around and in a moment he's into the hole. Prevention has failed. Although he had correctly identified the hazard while scouting, his paddling technique wasn't quite good enough. Now let's see how well he read the section on hole surfing. Whoops! A quick look at the upside-down boat tells the story. Now it becomes a question of rescue.

Most river-rescue situations are like this one: simple and uncomplicated. The paddler in this situation is in little danger, provided he is prepared and uses his head. A look at some dangerous situations is in order now, along with a quick review of river hazards and ways of dealing with them.

DROWNING. The most obvious threat to life on the water is drowning. A life jacket prevents this on calm water, but in turbulent water no life jacket can keep a swimmer's head above water all the time. Though strong swimming ability is a definite asset, it's really more important to be comfortable in the water. If you wear your life jacket, you can kick your way to shore whether you can swim well or not.

On large rivers with cold water (we are primarily speaking here of rivers west of the Mississippi), people sometimes die from *flush drowning,* a gasping reflex that causes them to aspirate water while swimming through big waves in cold water. For most canoeists, however, hypothermia (discussed in more detail below) is more of a danger. Few paddlers actually die of hypothermia; rather, it is very often a contributing factor in drowning, since it steals a swimmer's strength. This is particularly true of paddlers over forty years old. Beware of situations in which there is 1) very cold water, 2) a warm, sunny day, and 3) a potentially long swim on a wide river or a big lake. You are soon sweating, and the temptation to strip down is almost irresistible. Swimming even a hundred yards in conditions like this is much harder than you think, and a number of people haven't made it. Even strong swimmers have inexplicably vanished. It is sometimes called the *sudden disappearance syndrome.* The solution is to dress for the *water,* or to keep the boat close enough to shore that your swim will be short.

ENTRAPMENTS. On shallow, rocky rivers (such as those found in the eastern United States), the main peril to lift is *entrapment,* being held underwater or in the water by the force of the current. This usually happens after an extremity is caught, but a person's whole body is also subject to entrapment. *Foot entrapment* is common: a person's foot gets wedged into a crevice or under a rock in the riverbed, and the force of the current pushes him into it and keeps him there. This force can be overpowering, making escape or rescue difficult. (We'll talk about how to deal with the situation below.) A paddler can also become entrapped when his boat folds or wraps. This is less likely in an open canoe than in a decked boat, but it is still possible. In a recent incident on the Ocoee River, a paddler was entrapped in a wrapped open canoe for over forty-five minutes. He escaped only when rescuers sawed the boat in half to release him.

A broach occurs when a boat is pushed sideways into a rock by the current.

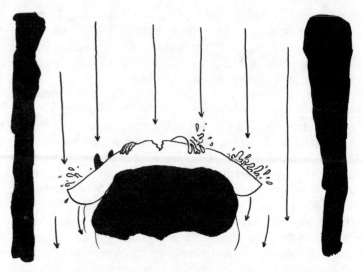

BROACHES AND PINS. Normally, we say that a boat is *pinned*, and a person is entrapped. A boat may be *broached* when pushed sideways into an obstacle and wrapped or held there by the force of the current, or it may be *vertically pinned* when coming off a drop. In a vertical pin the bow of the boat slams down into the riverbed, and water flowing over the ledge behind it keeps it from washing off. Of the two situations, broaches are far more common for canoes. Most are not life-threatening, although they may ruin your boat (and your day).

Prevention of broaches starts with avoiding obstacles. However, it's unrealistic to think that you'll miss them all, no matter how good you are. Since being broached is by definition being pushed sideways into a rock, try to stay out of that position. What usually happens is this: the paddler sees a rock dead ahead, turns to avoid it, and hits the rock sideways, broaching the boat (this is what happened to the *Titanic*). If you have a choice, it's better to ram the rock dead-on than to wash against it sideways.

However, if you can't avoid being swept sideways against it, *lean toward the rock*. Why? Think about what's happening to the boat. As it comes up against the rock, it stops moving downstream. The current now pushes against the upstream gunnel—the same situation as in a peel-out—so that unless you shift your weight downstream and apply a counterlean, the boat will flip upstream. Unfortunately, the instinctive reaction is to lean away from the rock that's rushing toward them. If the boat then flips upstream, suddenly the open side of the boat is in the water, facing the current like a big scoop. The boat swiftly fills with water, whose force pushes the ends around the rock. Even if the boat doesn't wrap, it may still be broached solidly in place by the force of the current and the weight of the water in the boat.

Now let's try that again. This time, shift your weight downstream and lean toward the rock. You may even grab on to the rock and hug it. The water is still pushing on the hull, but the current tends to slide under the boat and push it up toward the surface. You can now work your way along the face of the rock and push yourself off the side. Many times the river will do this for you—as long as you keep your downstream lean.

ROCKS. The danger of a rock is that it may entrap a paddler or broach a boat on the upstream side. The upstream face of a rock may be rounded or flat and have a cushion of water on the upstream side, which tends to deflect floating objects. But many undercut rocks do not have this cushion, making any object,

Lean into that rock! This decked canoeist has avoided a broach and is now trying to slide off the rock downstream.

boat, or person much more likely to wash up against them. If the undercut slopes downward, broached boats are much more likely to be forced underwater. Rescue from undercuts is difficult, dangerous, and beyond the scope of this book. Avoid them!

TIP: How can you identify an undercut? Water flowing into a rock should create a noticeable white cushion upstream. If not, suspect an undercut and stay away from the upstream side of the rock. Another sign is water boiling up behind the rock. If the cushion is behind rather than in front of the rock, beware. The converse, however, is not always true: a rock may have a cushion and still be undercut.

Boulder sieves are another, similar hazard. A series of boulders, dumped into the river by a landslide or a flash flood, often forms a rapid. The danger is that these boulders act like a sieve, sifting out solid objects like boats. Like undercuts and strainers, boulder sieves are extremely dangerous and should be avoided.

STRAINERS. Strainers are a common hazard in forested areas. As the river undercuts the banks on the outside of a bend, trees may topple into the water. Strainers work just as the name implies: they pose no barrier for water but strain out people and canoes. Canoes can also easily broach on tree trunks. Avoid strainers; to prepare for them, read about self-rescue.

DEBRIS. Some rivers are dumps, full of debris ranging from old cars and washing machines to rebar and broken dams. This type of trash is not only dangerous but sometimes hard to spot. Be especially careful around rivers like this, and play elsewhere if possible.

HOLES, HYDRAULICS, AND LOW-HEAD DAMS. These, along with rocks, are the most common river hazards. Put enough water over a rock and it becomes a hole. The large, economy-size holes can easily flip a boat and will usually wash out boats and paddlers in short order. If you're not prepared for the swim and the ensuing rescue, you may have difficulties. Hydraulics, which have an upstream current, cause more problems, since the backwash will hold (and recirculate) a buoyant object like a boat or person. Most naturally formed hydraulics have some breaks or weak spots in them for escapes. However, man-made hydraulics, such as low-head dams, do not; escape from these innocuous-looking killers is difficult or impossible.

For the sake of convenience, however, we're going to use the term *hole* here more or less interchangeably with *hydraulic*. If you're trying to get out, it matters little which one you're in.

First, learn to identify holes and hydraulics, both from the bank while scouting (look for the backwash) and from the boat (look for a horizon line). Then try to avoid them. If this fails, try to escape, using the techniques we discussed in chapter 6. A hole is normally weakest on the sides, where the upstream current from the hole meets the downstream river current. However, there may be other breaks or weak spots in the backwash that permit escape.

TIP: How friendly is that hole? Like people, some holes are friendly and some are not. Does it smile or frown at you? Look at the corners. Do the corners curve downstream? If so, the hole is "smiling" and will be easier to get out of. In a smiling hole, water at the corners tends to blend with the downstream current. Thus, as you work your way to the sides, this type of hole offers less resistance to getting out. A "frowning" hole, on the other hand, can be a problem. Here the corners of the hole point upstream; its ends are steeper and less likely to merge with the downstream current. Most of the water in a frowning hole flows back toward the center of the hole, which means you'll have to work against it to get out.

Worst of all is a steep hole, radically curved like a horseshoe. All the water flows back into the center of the hole, making escape nearly impossible. Smiling or frowning means little here; to the experienced water reader, this hole is gnashing its teeth! Stay away.

After avoidance fails, or if you deliberately choose to surf a hole and want to get out, you must first get to the weakest point of the hole. In previous chapters we learned how to surf a hole by shifting our weight and

In a "smiling" hole, the water tends to flow out of the corners of the hole, making escape easier. In a frowning hole, however, the water tends to flow back into the center of the hole, making escape more difficult.

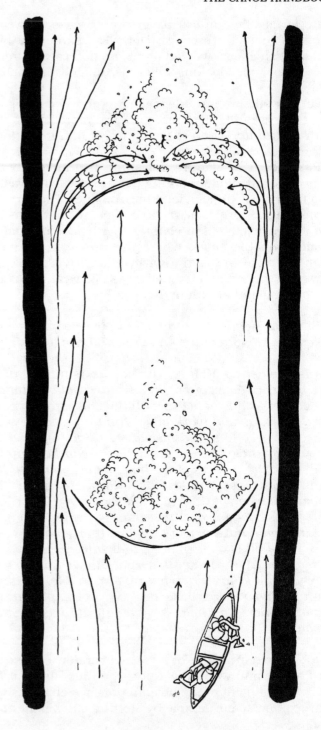

leaning the boat downstream. Now comes the payoff. If you just sit there with your weight on a low brace, you won't be able to move around. Maybe the hole will choose to spit you out, maybe it won't . . .

Although many enthusiastic paddlers just jump into a hole and then try to figure out how to leave, it's better to check out the hole first. Are there obvious weak points in the backwash? What about the ends? Does one end look easier to escape from than the other? Is there a convenient eddy for getting in and out? And most important: what happens if you fill up with water, or if you have to swim out? Are there obstacles or rapids downstream? If so, you might want to choose another hole to play in.

Moving back and forth in a hole is simple. Use either a forward stroke or a back stroke. The same principles apply here as on flat water: use your torso for power. For a canoeist in a hole, the most powerful stroke is the back stroke. Plant the blade behind you and rotate your torso to pull the canoe backward out of the hole. A forward stroke works also, but it isn't quite as powerful.

Say you've worked your way to the end of the hole and still can't get out. Oops. Now what? Maybe a little momentum will help. Most holes are dynamic in the sense that a boat in them will be moved back and forth by the natural action of the water. As with other river forces, you can use this to your advantage. As the water starts moving you toward the ends of the hole, use a good hard stroke to accelerate the process. That extra momentum may make the difference. When you reach the hole's edge, *then* plant the paddle in the downstream current moving past the hole, and hang on. You may have to try this several times, rocking back and forth until you get enough momentum to escape.

One other thing that's usually a little disconcerting may happen at this point. You can very easily get spun around in some holes and end up on your off side. This usually happens at the corner of a hole while you're trying to escape. Now it's easy to say that off-side moves (cross forward strokes and cross back strokes) work just the same as on-side moves, and they do. But for most canoeists, an off-side surf really isn't an op-

THE PROBE

Probing a hole or rapid is a ceremony somewhat akin to divining the future with the entrails of a chicken. Say you are in doubt as to whether to surf a certain hole. You choose a particularly naive, gullible, or trusting friend, and send him in first. After all, what are friends for? Of course, you tell the probe that you've done this hole many times before. After watching his progress (or demise), you decide. When the friend (if indeed he still is one) angrily approaches you, paddle in hand, for a confrontation, you simply shrug and innocently say, "Well, I guess the water must be up a little."

tion. Unless you're better than most, try switching hands so that the paddle stays on the downstream side of the boat.

Still in there? By now your open boat is probably starting to fill up with water. This can be good or bad, depending on the nature of the hole. In some very deep holes, a boat full of water makes escape more difficult. In a shallow hole, however, the boat may wash out after it fills with water. Once out of the hole, you'll quickly find that a water-filled boat is slow, heavy, and hard to manage, as well as more prone to pin. You've already picked a close haven to get into, right?

Suppose you're *still* in that hole. Okay, time for the big decision. You've tried A. You've tried B. But the hole hangs on to your boat like duct tape on a patch. Time to eject. Unlike a jet fighter, however, your canoe does not have a cannon shell under the seat to blast you free of trouble. You'll have to do it yourself, and your next few moves will be critical. Most holes have either a breaking wave or a surface backwash keeping the boat in. If this is the case, anything below the surface will quickly be carried downstream. If you come out of the boat, you also will be dragged away.

If you go, however, think about a few things beforehand. First, if the resulting swim will be long or difficult, don't sit in the hole until you're exhausted and have little reserve for self-rescue. Second, make sure you are free of any entangling ropes, thigh straps, and the like. Third, try to get over the backwash by diving over the gunnel on the downstream side. Pick a weak spot or do it at the edge of the hole. And finally, keep your eye on the boat. You want to stay away from it.

In a hydraulic with a deep backwash, however, you may be pulled back upstream into the hole. If so, you are in a very dangerous situation, not least because your boat is probably still in there, too. Swimming in a hydraulic with a water-filled canoe is an experience best left to the imagination. Such escape techniques as exist for this situation are described below.

Rescue

We now come to the last stage of the process that began with hazard identification. If you are unable to either avoid or deal with the hazard, it's time for rescue. Rescue is a big field, and here we'll have room to cover only the fundamentals. However, basic rescue skills, including swimming, are just as important as paddling skills.

First, some general considerations. Our primary goal in rescue is *not to make the would-be rescuer another victim*. Though you may choose to take a reasonable risk to save a life, don't make yourself another statistic. It follows, then, that you should not attempt a rescue if you will endanger yourself or others unreasonably. Make sure that you are able to back up other rescuers so that they don't get into trouble. And finally, rescue the victim.

Decide what kind of rescue to use. Self-rescue, obviously, comes first. Some types of rescues are extremely dangerous; others, like using a throw bag, are relatively safe. I strongly recommend that you take a river-rescue course as part of your general paddling education, and that you read *River Rescue* (see Resources), because here we have no room for anything but a beginning.

The safest place for you to be as a rescuer is on shore. You may slip and break a leg, but you won't drown. So start with a shore-based rescue, if possible. You may be able to pull someone to safety with a throw bag. The next best rescue is done by boat, usually by towing a swimmer to shore. By putting yourself on the water, however, you are now less safe, since your boat may overturn, making you another victim. Finally, there are swimming, or in-water, rescues. These are the most dangerous, since you're now in nearly the same fix as the victim. So the preferred sequence is shore-based, then boat-based rescue, and finally, if no other option exists, an in-water rescue. The old Red Cross mnemonic RETHROG helps us to remember this: REach, THrow, ROw, Go.

Positioning the rescuers is also important. They must be close enough to help without endangering themselves, and far enough downstream to take into account the speed of the current, since most river accidents take a few moments to get sorted out. A very common safety setup: two rescuers stand on the bank using throw bags to pull swimmers in, and boaters wait below to help get swimmers and gear to shore.

HOW MANY IS ENOUGH?
The American Whitewater Affili-ation recommends a minimum party of three craft. This is a good idea even on calm water. If an emergency develops with one boat, two others are standing by to assist. If someone is injured, one boat can stay while another goes for help.

These are mutually supporting systems. And if one fails, another takes over. For example, if a rope throw misses, a backup boat waiting farther down can res-cue the swimmer. On a drop-and-pool river (that is, a rapid followed by a calm spot), the rescuers set up with throw ropes just below the rapid and a boat or two in the pool. Though it seems obvious that people should be rescued before gear, this tenet has been ignored on a surprising number of occasions. If you have enough rescuers, let some rescuers go after the gear and some after people.

This all fits together with what we've said so far about trip leadership and organization. The group stops and scouts together. After deciding on routes (and whether to run), they next decide where and how to set safety. Usually, some paddlers walk down below the rapid and set up throw ropes. If the rapid is long and difficult, they may set them at different points in the rapid where hazards exist, so that a paddler who dumps won't have to swim the entire rapid. As soon as they're set up, the rope throwers signal to each other and to the waiting paddlers that they are ready. Now the strongest boats run through. Some of these paddlers may stay in their boats to be available for rescue, while others get out and take over the ropes, allowing the rope throwers to return to their boats. Now the weaker boats come through. If they dump, there is now an adequate safety net below to retrieve paddlers, boats, and gear. After the last boat comes through, the group heads downstream.

Self-Rescue

Of all forms of rescue, self-rescue is the most impor-tant. You can let the river have your boat, but you can't buy another life. Self-rescue begins with an attitude: *I can take care of myself on the river*. Ultimately, you are responsible for yourself. It is fine to have rescue backups, as we've described, but these sometimes fail. When they do, you must be able to rescue yourself, sometimes in difficult circumstances. Unfortunately, civilized life has made us dependent on the "system," on an assumption that someone, from the 911 Good Guys to passing boaters, will rescue us. Thus it's not unusual these days to see boaters floating through a rapid, looking for someone to help them as if it were a matter of course. If you choose to paddle, you owe it to the rest of the river community not to burden others with rescuing you unless it is a true emergency. You also owe it to others to take some care about what you do; river rescue is dangerous, and if you have to be rescued, you will be risking others' lives. There are too many stories of people who carelessly got themselves into trouble, then took a couple of rescuers with them.

Now it's time to talk about being in the river without a boat—an essential skill. Flatwater rivers sometimes flood, making whitewater self-rescue skills necessary even if you live in Kansas. Open canoeists will probably get more practice with swimming self-rescue than their friends in decked boats. Anyway, even if you can roll an open canoe, there will be times when you either choose to swim or have no choice.

When swimming a rapid, a paddler uses the same techniques as when in a boat. The basic mechanics of the situation have not changed—swimmers still use eddy turns, peel-outs, and ferries. But the object *is* different. When swimming, you generally want to get out of the water and over to shore as soon as you can, preferably with all your gear. (There are exceptions, and where the river is wide or perhaps very cold, you may want to do a self-rescue in the river using techniques we'll consider below.)

Swimming is potentially more dangerous than paddling. Your moves will be much slower than in a boat, making it harder to avoid hazards. Since you're almost at eye level with the river, you can't see very far. Breathing can be a problem among big waves. And finally, with most of your body down in the water, you run a greater risk of entrapment. Sounds grim, doesn't it? Take heart. People do it all the time without problems. Like anything else in boating, there are right and wrong ways (here meaning safe and unsafe ways) to do it.

On shallow, rocky rivers, the main danger is entrapment of an extremity, usually a foot. This happens most often when a person tries to stand up in moving water. Swimmers can prevent foot entrapment by keeping their feet near the surface of the water in the so-called safe swimming position. Here the swimmer faces downstream, lying more or less on his back with his feet up. This keeps him near the surface of the water and allows him to look downstream and fend off rocks with his feet. However, it's not a very efficient swimming position, since it allows the swimmer to use only a backstroke. When the water deepens, as it usually does in the pool below a rapid, a crawl stroke or side stroke gets you in to shore faster. The key is to swim aggressively and not just float through a rapid. The bigger the rapids, and the colder and wider the river, the more important it is to get in to shore quickly.

On deep rivers, where the danger of foot entrapment is minimal (most foot entrapments occur in waist-deep or shallower water), it's okay to use a crawl stroke right away to get over to shore. Swimming through big waves requires you to time your breathing so that you inhale in the trough rather than in the wave crest.

The other exception to swimming feet-first is when you are unable to avoid a strainer. If you are swept into a log or tree trunk feet first, your chances of being pushed under it are very good. To avoid this, you must gain enough speed to get on top of the strainer. As you near the strainer, go from a feet-first to a head-first position, and swim as fast as possible toward the strainer. As you hit it, pull yourself up out of the water as quickly as you can and try to climb on top of it. At the very least, try to get as much of your body out of the water as possible.

Dressing for a swim is important, too. If the water is

When crossing a strainer, face downstream and swim towards it, then lift yourself over it.

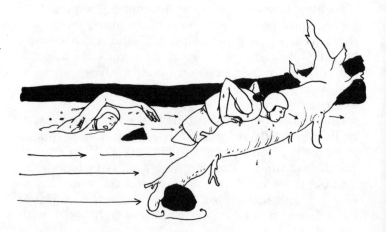

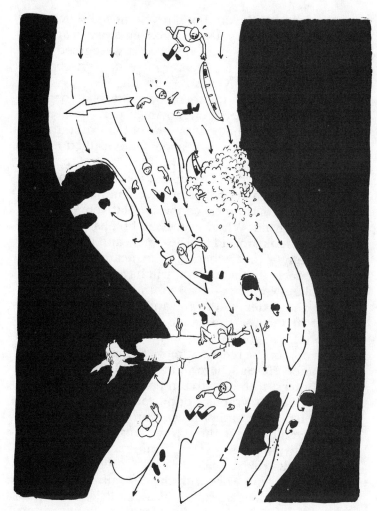

Swimming strategy. Try to hang on to your gear, but don't hesitate to ditch it if necessary. Swim feet-first except when crossing a strainer or when in deep water where you can use a face-first crawl stroke to get into an eddy and then to shore.

warm and the swim short, no more than a bathing suit for decency and a life jacket for flotation is required. But a long swim in cold water can quickly sap a swimmer's strength. Remember, only a wetsuit or drysuit will protect you while actually in the water.

And finally, swimming, like any other boating skill, requires practice. As a novice, you'll get plenty, but don't forget self-rescue skills as you move up the paddling ladder to more difficult water.

SWIMMING WITH A BOAT. Swimming by yourself is one thing, but add a boat and you're in another

situation entirely. If you thought you moved slowly before, wait until you try it with a sixteen-foot sea anchor
dragging you downstream. However, we agreed that
you are responsible for recovering your own gear. It
isn't impossible, but it is more difficult.

Whether you attempt to recover the boat or not,
once you have dumped it on moving water, you need to
know where it is. The boat is now full of water and at
the mercy of the current. Since a water-filled canoe
weighs a ton, literally, you'll want to stay upstream of
it. Remember the forces we talked about in chapter 1?
You don't want to get between a rock and that kind of
power. Still, a swamped canoe is relatively sluggish
and easy to avoid. When your head breaks water after
a spill, first look around for the canoe, and then glance
downstream to see where you're headed. If you've
already checked this out, you will have some idea of a
rescue plan. Now assume a swimming position that's
safe for the water you're in, and decide whether to
attempt to recover the canoe or to abandon it and
strike out for shore immediately.

If you opt for the recovery, move to the upstream end
of the canoe. Here's where you want to be able to get at
your painters. If the upstream painter is floating free,
grab it (but *don't* wrap it around your wrist or hand). If
it's not, fish it out and promise yourself you'll make it
more accessible next time. Now start swimming the
boat over to shore as best you can. Ferry the boat over
using a backstroke or sidestroke, looking for eddies to
land in, and try to work with the current. Keeping the
boat pointing downstream will make it less likely to
pin. If at any time things start looking chancy, ditch
the boat and head for shore.

Hang on to your paddle, too. Here you'll be glad you
tied everything in securely and don't have any trailing
lines (except the painters) to worry about.

TIP: *If you flip the boat over right-side-up, it is much
easier to pull, especially if it has a fair amount of
flotation in it. If the boat is upright, sometimes it
works just as well to give the boat a good shove
toward the riverbank, then swim after it, shoving it
as required. This works equally well whether you
are doing a swimming rescue or a boat-based rescue.*

The Capistrano Flip: the paddlers swim underneath the boat and toss it up out of the water.

FLATWATER SELF-RESCUE. So far we've talked about moving-water rescue. Rescue on small bodies of flat water is similar, but larger bodies of water, such as big lakes and wide rivers, call for different techniques.

On narrow, sluggish rivers it's easy to swim a boat over, even if it has no flotation. However, if you are a mile from shore, swimming the boat may not be a workable option. This is especially true when the water is cold and hypothermia is a problem. If rescue seems imminent, you will probably want to stay with the swamped boat. It provides some flotation and can sometimes even be paddled. If the wait is likely to be a long one, you must decide whether to conserve body heat and energy or attempt an in-water self-rescue.

If you decide to wait it out, try to minimize heat loss by moving as little as possible. Recent studies have shown that you'll last longer by not moving than by trying to generate heat. Exercise does generate heat, but you will lose it faster, too. A better idea is to adopt the help or huddle postures, which can reduce heat loss by up to 35 percent.

The most obvious in-water self-rescue is swimming to shore. Before setting out for a long swim, however, try turning the swamped boat back upright and rocking some of the water out of it. If this succeeds and you are able to reenter the boat, you can bail out much of the remaining water with a paddle. Kneel in the boat and begin flicking water over the gunnel with the paddle blade until the boat is manageable again. A third method is the Capistrano Flip (see sidebar). The flip is easiest with an unloaded canoe and two people. One

THE CAPISTRANO FLIP

The Capistrano Flip is a useful self-rescue technique. It works best with unloaded tandem canoes. The paddlers turn their swamped canoe upside down, then swim underneath and come up under the boat, lifting it. They rock the boat back and forth to break the slight vacuum formed when the water empties out. On a signal, both paddlers give a quick scissors kick to stabilize themselves and toss the boat into an upright position. If they do it quickly enough, they should be able to keep most of the water out of the boat as it flips over. Holding on to a gunnel, one paddler stabilizes the boat so that the other paddler can climb in over the gunnel on the other side. This paddler then takes his paddle and leans his weight onto a low brace over the gunnel while his partner climbs aboard. This is pretty similar to the confidence lean (chapter 3). He does this by doing a quick pullup on the gunnel (assisted by a scissors kick). As his butt clears the gunnel, he twists and slides onto the bottom of the canoe.

With practice, the Capistrano Flip can be done quickly and effectively, even in Class II white water.

person can do it, but he will find it difficult to get back in the boat unassisted (this is another reason for multiboat parties). Practice it near shore—it isn't *quite* as easy as it looks. Canoe trippers who anticipate using this technique may want to rig their load so that it can be released when the need for a flip arises.

Boat Rescues

Almost every paddler ends up making boat rescues. A rescue boat is often very quick to get on the scene. It can operate on rivers too wide for a throw rope. But you need to be able to paddle the water that you'll be making the rescue in. Otherwise, it's very easy to end up as another victim. Open canoes, being easy to swamp, have definite limitations as rescue boats, and solo canoes are relatively slow. This limits them, for the most part, to easier water. That's not to say that they can't be used effectively (after all, the pool below a Class V rapid may be totally flat), just that it takes some planning and common sense.

Do not, for example, blindly take off after someone without knowing what's downriver. Do back up rescue boats with rescue ropes if possible, and decide in advance who goes for gear and who for swimmers. People come first, but because of the problems inherent in using open canoes to rescue swimmers, it's often better to let the ropes catch them, while the boaters go after boats and paddles.

Still, you will at some point probably have to pick up a swimmer. This isn't always safe or easy. Victims sometimes panic, and if someone comes crawling over the gunnel, you will have a hard time staying upright. Approach swimmers with caution. Sometimes it's enough just to provide moral support as they swim for shore. Other times they'll need help. If you are in a position to help safely, toss out the stern painter for the swimmer to grab and head for shore. The swimmer can help by kicking to reduce the amount of drag on the boat. Your canoe will nevertheless be incredibly slow and sluggish, and the anchor on the stern will keep turning the boat upstream. Misjudge this and your boat will be in danger. If it happens, you may have to jettison the swimmer—if he will let go!

Rescuing boats requires a different technique. The most common one is the bulldozer, in which one or more boats nudge a swamped boat into shore like tug-boats. This can be slow, and it doesn't work very well in swift water. Flip the canoe upright to make this task easier. If the boat is not totally swamped, sometimes a good push toward shore will be all that's needed.

Some paddlers tow a boat by wrapping a painter around a thwart and holding the wrap with pressure from the knee or thigh. This is fine *if* you can release the line when need be. Never tie a swamped boat to your own.

Boat rescue is especially difficult in white water. Many clinics and clubs have students practice boat rescue along with other paddling techniques. This sometimes results in a mass of upside-down boats floating downriver, but it prepares these paddlers to make rescues on harder water.

FLATWATER BOAT RESCUE. All the techniques we've mentioned so far work well on flat water. However, there is one method—boat-over-boat rescue—that's pretty much limited to flat water, either on big lakes or extremely wide rivers. Boat-over-boat simply uses other craft as a platform from which to dump water from the swamped canoe and get its paddlers back in it.

Boat-over-boat obviously requires having at least one rescue boat. Two or more boats work better, since they can provide additional stability. The paddlers turn the swamped boat upside down and pull it over the rescue boat, emptying out the water. Then, balancing it on their gunnels, they turn the boat right side up and slide it back into the water. The rescuers hold the gunnels of the emptied boat, allowing the paddlers to climb in from the other side. Provided the rescuers have enough skill to keep from dumping themselves, this works well.

Rope Rescue

For most canoeists, "rope" means a throw bag: a nylon sack containing a foam float into which is stuffed a length of polypropylene rope. This is the most common and necessary rescue tool on the river. Every paddler should carry a throw bag *and* know how to use it. A misused throw rope can be a dangerous tool to both the rescuer and the victim. Why? Ropes and water form a potentially lethal combination if someone gets entangled in the water and can't get free. So a few safety rules are in order. First, *never* tie anyone—victim or rescuer—to a rope, either in the water or on the bank. Second, if you work with or around ropes, carry an easily accessible knife to cut the rope if necessary. Third, make sure the bag is secured in your boat so that it doesn't spew rope all over if you abandon ship. Fourth, take the time to know when and how to use a throw rope; follow the guidelines below. Fifth, practice enough to keep that proficiency current. Throwing ability falls off rapidly with disuse, and you may not notice it until you miss a critical throw.

*Safety setup. The rope thrower at **A** is too far upstream to effectively reach a swimmer who dumps in the chute, although he might be able to rescue someone out of the hydraulic on river left. A chase boat below the drop is a good backup, but he should avoid getting pulled into the rapid below. A rope at **B** is more effective to retrieve the swimmer. The rope at **C** is in a good position, and covers the swimmer from being swept into the undercut rock below. However, there is no convenient eddy in which to swing the swimmer. **D** is an excellent place for a rope and has a good eddy below. It is also a good location for a chase boat backup. The photographer at **E** cannot shoot and throw at the same time. The rope thrower at **F** has a good eddy in which to pull the swimmer, but the throw is a long one. The chase boat is probably a better option here, especially if there is a pool below.*

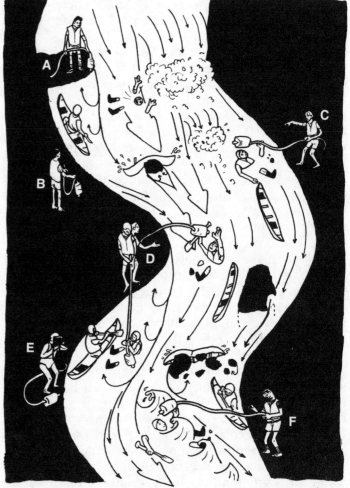

After Jan Atlee © 1990

Rope rescue is the primary form of shore-based rescue for paddlers. It is relatively safe for the rescuer and quick to deploy. The disadvantages are that it is limited by the length of the rope (the practical limit is about fifty feet) to narrow rivers. Rope rescue, though, also integrates well with other systems, like rescue boats.

Where do you set ropes? Normally, one or more of the paddlers walks down below a difficult rapid, or to a convenient spot along it. To choose his spot, the rope thrower needs to do several things:

• Allow some space for a paddler to perceive what's happening after a spill. Set up a bit downstream of where an accident is likely to happen. If you're too close, the victim may not have time to realize what's going on—or may still be underwater—when you throw. How far downstream will depend on the nature of the rapid and the speed of the current.

• Pick a place to land the victim. When he catches the rope, he will make a pendulum swing in from the current to a point below the rescuer. Ideally, this should put him in an eddy, or at least somewhere out of the main current. The pool below a rapid is a good place, but in the case of a long rapid, you may choose to place several ropes at different points.

• Set up a rescue system in depth. Unless the rapid is very easy, back up your ropes, either with another rope farther down or with another rescue system, like a boat. If possible, station the ropes far enough away from each other so that they won't interfere with each other by getting entangled on the fly or, worse, around the victim.

• Consider what will happen when the rope goes taut with a victim on the end. The rescuer should have a firm stance or, better, room to move a bit downstream to cushion the shock (a dynamic belay). Often it helps to have another paddler on hand to assist.

• Ask whether the spot allows a clear throw. Are there brush, wires, trees, or anything that will interfere?

ROPE THROWING. Most paddlers use the underhand throw, which works well for most purposes. (Rope throwing is discussed in greater detail in *River Rescue*.) The thrower opens the mouth of the bag about halfway, pulls out a foot or so of rope to hold in

The underhand rope throw: wind up . . .

and throw.

his nonthrowing hand, then swings the bag behind him, letting go as it comes forward. It requires practice and fairly precise timing to reach the target. It's easy to throw short, so the best throw is one that aims beyond the victim and lays the rope over him.

Since the target is moving, the thrower must also lead the target, or the rope will fall behind the victim. Like shooting skeet, you probably won't get a hit the first time you try this. Swimmers tend to be preoccupied with their immediate situation, so you'll

The body belay. By wrapping the rope around her body, this paddler generates enough friction to belay a swimmer. She may increase friction by pulling her brake (left) hand in towards her body. Wearing a life-jacket reduces the chances of rope burns.

BELAYING

It's not easy, holding a rope with a person clinging to the other end. You'll want to find some way to *belay* yourself on shore. Belaying is a way of using the friction of the rope to add holding power. The most common form is the body belay, in which the rope thrower uses his body to provide friction. He first throws the rope. Then, before the rope becomes taut, he slips it behind himself around his waist. Holding the rope around his body provides enough friction to keep the rope from being jerked out of his hands, but still allows him to release it if necessary. For additional holding power he can sit behind a rock and push against it with his feet. Or several friends can pile on top of him.

Wear your life jacket (and gloves, if you have them) to reduce the possibility of rope burns. And grasp the short end of the rope (the end without the bag) with the *upstream* hand. This will make the belay open against your body as the swimmer goes past. Otherwise the rope will wrap around you.

If your life jacket has a built-in rescue harness, you may clip yourself to a tree with a carabiner and a sling (an exception to the no-tie rule, since the harness can easily be released), and then use a normal body belay. You may also belay by wrapping the rope once or twice around a fixed object like a tree, but *don't* tie it off.

The correct and incorrect ways to hold a throw rope while in the water. The second way results in a faceful of water.

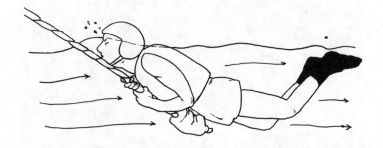

STATIC VS. DYNAMIC BELAYS
Belays can be either static or dynamic. A static belay is generally more secure, but it puts more loading shock on the swimmer when the rope becomes taut. This may cause the swimmer to let go of the rope. A dynamic belay reduces this shock. Here, the belayer progressively releases some of the tension by letting the rope slide through his hands in a body belay (rope burns can be a problem) or moving down the shore as the tension on the rope increases, loading it gradually. If you have a choice, use a dynamic belay.

want to get their attention before you throw. Yelling "Roooooope!" usually gets the job done.

Once the swimmer gets the rope, he needs to know what to do. The tendency is to grab the rope and roll over to face the rope thrower. As the swimmer gets swung around by the current, however, he will end up facing upstream with the water rushing directly into his face. Not only is this uncomfortable, it may cause him to let go. If he hangs on and ducks his head, his body may dive. Instead, the swimmer should roll over on his back, facing away from the rope thrower and belayer. This way the water flows against his back and tends to push him toward the surface. Even in a very swift current, an air pocket will form around the victim's head, allowing him to breathe. Finally, throw only one rope at a time. Overenthusiastic rescuers sometimes fill the air with ropes, creating a tangled and dangerous mess.

Boat Recovery

So far we've dealt with recovering free-floating boats. There will be times, however, when a boat gets pinned or broached on an obstacle, usually a rock. Then you'll have to get it off. For more complete coverage of boat recovery, refer to *River Rescue*.

You can often avoid pins by using proper technique, such as remembering to lean into rocks. Even if you avoid this fate, however, you still need to know something about boat recovery to help someone else.

Before we talk about technique, there are a few general safety considerations for unpinning boats. Because the pinned boat will most likely be full of water and very heavy, you want to be extremely careful. Boats can and do shift unpredictably, and have the potential to pin a foot or leg. Take a minute to think about what will happen when you get the boat free. Where will it go? If you are standing directly behind it, it may well run you over. A lot of boats have gone from a moderate pin to a really bad one after being pulled free from the first pin, or have simply disappeared downstream because no one considered the next step.

Unpinning a boat often puts the rescuers in the water, so think about that, too. What happens if one of them loses his footing and washes downstream? Obviously, someone should be standing by downstream of the accident site with a throw bag. If you are rigging ropes to the boat, do they pose a danger to other paddlers? Maybe you should put someone upstream of the accident site as well to warn approaching boaters. Does the pinned boat itself create a new hazard on the river? If so, especially if you can't recover it, you should either mark it or report it to the local rangers or river-managing agency.

Unless someone is actually pinned in it, there is seldom a rush to recover a boat. Choose the safest rather than the fastest method of recovery. On a dam-controlled river you can often use the absolutely safest and easiest method of boat recovery: just wait for the water to be shut off. Sometimes dam keepers are willing to do this in an emergency. Other times, you'll have to wait for the schedule.

In boat recovery, just as in paddling, you play a game with the water—trying to make its force work for and not against you. This time, however, the forces are much more obvious. Let's look at the forces in a typical canoe broach. Almost always, the open side of the canoe will end up turned upstream, with the water forcing the boat against a rock located somewhere near the center of the boat. Two forces are at work here: the push of the current against the hull (a dynamic force) and the weight of the water in the boat (a static force). The current pushes more or less equally across the surface of the hull. If we can somehow either reduce the weight of the boat or change the balance of the force on the hull, the boat will be easier to

The river's force is more or less equalized on both ends of a pinned boat. By lifting one end, the paddler upsets the equilibrium and is able to push the boat off.

recover. The river itself may move it off without any more intervention from us.

Reducing the weight starts with flotation. The higher a boat rides after a spill, the less likely it is to pin. The more water the flotation displaces, the less the boat will weigh when it does get swamped or pinned. But in any case, it will have some water in it. To reduce the weight, you can raise part of the canoe. You may do this by lifting one end, or by rolling the canoe over so that the open side of the canoe no longer faces upstream, then lifting the entire boat up. This second method is difficult to manage without some kind of haul system on the boat to first reduce the force pushing on it.

Lifting either one end or the whole boat also reduces the force of the current on the hull, so this is usually the first thing to try. If we can somehow make the current push harder on one end of the boat, the hull will tend to pivot around (or off) the obstacle that pinned it, even if it is badly wrapped.

Most boats can be recovered using the Armstrong Method: just pulling on the boat. This can be surprisingly effective if you know what you're doing. Get out to the boat by wading or paddling. Then analyze the situation. Start with whichever end looks easier to get to. Try lifting it. If possible, try to roll the boat over at the same time to dump the water out, and don't forget to secure it, with a rope if necessary, so that it doesn't take off downriver on its own.

Another way to upset the balance of forces on a pinned canoe is to attach a rope to one end and pull, either to lift it or to pull against the current and thereby cancel some of the river's force. You can generate a surprising amount of force just by putting a lot of people on the end of a rope. After all, that's how they built the pyramids. This is usually referred to as the Ten Boy Scout Method. Just keep adding people until the canoe moves or something breaks.

Speaking of breaking, you'll want to take some care in attaching the rope to the canoe. Canoe manufacturers do not design their boats to withstand such pulling and prying. The most obvious places to attach a rope—seats and thwarts—are also among the weakest parts of the boat, particularly if made of wood. The

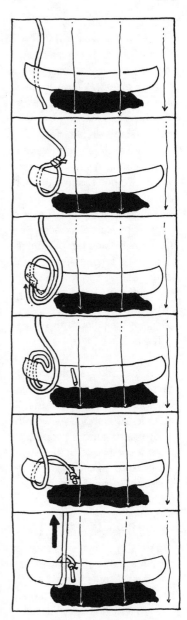

The Steve Thomas Rope Trick is a handy way of rigging a pinned boat.

WATER WALKING

The danger of wading is foot entrapment, but you can reduce the danger by multiplying the number of legs you use. In fairly slow or shallow water, use a paddle: three legs—a tripod—are more stable than two. Face upstream and lean your weight on the paddle held in front of you. Move one foot (or the paddle) at a time, crabbing your way across the current. If more people are available, place them behind and beside you in a *wedge*. The second person stands slightly behind and to one side of you, holding on to your life jacket and facing upstream. Your paddle is the point of the wedge.

The *people pivot* requires at least two people. Stand facing each other and grab the shoulders of each other's life jackets. One person moves while the other lends support. As with the wedge, adding more people increases stability. The pivot works by rotating while moving across the current. The person farthest upstream forms the pivot. He braces against the current and the rest of the group rotates around him until another person assumes the upstream position. Then *he* braces, becomes the pivot, and so on.

If you have a choice, select a fairly shallow crossing and move from eddy to eddy. If the pivot or wedge fails, everyone lets go and practices self-rescue. Cover a crossing with a throw rope if possible.

bow and stern plates are stronger, and the hull is stronger still. A clever solution to the problem of lifting and dumping the boat at the same time is to encircle the hull with a rope so that it pulls the boat up and rotates it, dumping the water. To do this, the rope is attached to the thwart nearest the bottom of the river, then wrapped underneath the hull and run upstream. The rope is tied to the thwart but does not pull directly on it; instead, the thwart merely locates the end of the rope, and the force is taken by the hull. The rescuers then pull so that the rope rotates the boat upstream and dumps the water. If everything works out, the boat ends up nearly empty on the water's surface and can be pulled to shore.

But attaching a rope to the bottom thwart isn't always so easy in the river. To make it work, you have to push the rope underneath the boat against the current. Fortunately, someone figured out a better way. It is the Steve Thomas Rope Trick, named after one of its first practitioners. Pass the rope under the boat downstream, which is much easier, and then rotate the rope around the boat into the proper position for hauling.

Generally the sequence of events for dealing with a pinned boat goes something like this: analyze the situation, then try to muscle the boat off by lifting the ends. If that fails, try attaching a rope and finding some Boy Scouts to pull on it. If that doesn't work, find someone who's taken a river-rescue course and knows how to set up a mechanical haul system.

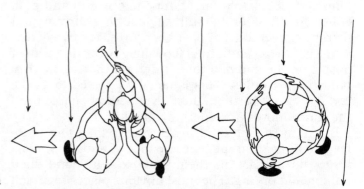

Wading. The group on the left forms a wedge, while the group on the right forms a "people pivot." With mutual support, surprisingly deep water can be forded.

Some medical problems on the river, like drowning, can be fatal and simple, but most are just plain simple. Paddlers generally are not subject to the severe traumatic injuries of, say, climbers. Nevertheless, all paddlers should take at least a basic first-aid course. Since drowning is the biggest threat to life on any body of water, a course in cardiopulmonary resuscitation (CPR), renewed yearly, should be considered mandatory. If your paddling takes you to the far reaches of the wilderness, or anywhere that may put you an hour or more from medical aid, take a more advanced course that includes instruction in prolonged care and treatment. Few things are more frustrating than having an injured friend (or being injured yourself) and having neither the knowledge nor the equipment to do anything about it. The National Association of Search and Rescue (see Resources) offers a Wilderness First Responder Course, which includes instruction in prolonged care and transport. It is certainly something any wilderness tripper or whitewater paddler should consider taking.

DROWNING. There is little to say about drowning except that you should avoid it using the safety techniques we've covered so far. If a member of your party drowns, you must rescue him, start CPR, and attempt to get him medical attention as soon as you can. A few wilderness rules apply, however. Both hypothermia and cold-water near-drowning syndrome can, in some situations, prolong a person's life underwater, so start CPR even if a victim has been submerged for up to an hour. Then continue until medical support arrives, the victim starts breathing on his own, or you become exhausted or are endangering yourself or members of your party.

HYPOTHERMIA. Hypothermia is the cooling of the body. Dress properly and keep up your body's reserves of fuel by eating and drinking adequately for cold conditions. Hypothermia affects a person's judgment, so keep an eye on your friends. If they are cold and start acting irrationally (admittedly, this is hard to tell with many paddlers), suspect hypothermia.

Otherwise, recognizing hypothermia is fairly easy: the person starts to shiver and acts cold. Often this is enough to affect a person's paddling ability, which can

Medical

lead to repeated swims. If this happens to you or a member of your party, stop and warm up. Eat and drink something, put on some dry clothes (which you have brought along for just such a situation as this), or if necessary build a fire. If conditions are really inclement, you may want to call off the trip. Wilderness trippers don't have this option and must be prepared to make a storm-proof camp.

So far we've been talking about *wind-chill* hypothermia. This form of hypothermia is gradual and insidious, and is characterized by a gradual, progressive cooling of the body's core. More dangerous to paddlers is *immersion* hypothermia. Since water sucks heat out of the body more than thirty times as fast as air, the water doesn't have to be terribly cold to induce hypothermia—about 70°F is cold enough, especially if it is moving past you. Immersion hypothermia happens in a hurry, cooling the extremities and making swimming difficult or impossible. The good side of this situation is that the body's core remains relatively warm, so that a swimmer's chances of recovery are very good *if* he is rescued.

Severe hypothermia starts, roughly, when shivering stops. This is a sign of real trouble—a dangerous, life-threatening condition. A person with severe hypothermia may act irrationally or lapse into unconsciousness. He may even appear to be dead, with no pulse or respiration detectable in the field. Your only course of action in this situation is to insulate the person as well as possible to conserve remaining body heat, and transport him to a hospital. Some cautions apply. Handle the victim gently; rough treatment may cause the heart to beat uncontrollably and lead to death. Do not try to rewarm a severely hypothermic person in the field—this requires specialized equipment. The body goes into a metabolic icebox—almost a state of suspended animation—and can survive for a surprisingly long time in this condition.

SHOULDER DISLOCATIONS. Less common among canoeists than among kayakers, a dislocated shoulder is caused by the ball of the upper arm popping out of the socket of the shoulder. It is a painful and disabling injury, and it usually happens when a paddler's arm gets behind him and receives a sharp blow, as when the paddle hits a rock.

To avoid shoulder dislocations, practice good paddling technique. Specifically, keep your hands in the box. As long as your arms are in front of you, your shoulders are pretty safe. Relocating a shoulder, though not difficult, is a job for a medically trained person. However, if you or a paddling companion have had a dislocation in the past, or if you are planning to venture into remote areas, you may want to have a doctor show you how to relocate a shoulder.

MINOR INJURIES. Treat minor injuries—cuts, scrapes, and bruises—with normal first-aid procedures. Two common but preventable boating injuries are sunburn and blisters. Another very common injury is tendinitis, an irritation and swelling of the sheath around a tendon. For canoeists this usually happens in the tendons of the forearms. Tendinitis can take what seems like forever to heal. It is caused by overuse, and a common way of getting it is to start paddling hard after a long layoff, or without having had an exercise program beforehand. Tendinitis can be treated with ice, ibuprofen, and rest, but it's better avoided altogether. Keep up your exercise program, stretch before paddling, and warm up gradually on easy water.

EVACUATIONS. If you are boating on a river inside a city (say, on the James River in Richmond) your first-aid kit may consist of little more than change to call an ambulance, which can then drive down to the water's edge to pick up the injured person. If, however, you are in a remote, steep-walled gorge laced with Classes V and VI rapids, or crossing the Barren Lands in northern Canada, evacuations will be a bit harder.

Due to space limitations, we cannot discuss subjects like spinal management, litters, and backboards. Fortunately, most of the evacuations you will be faced with will be relatively simple. Many rivers have roads alongside, since river gorges were often convenient places to build them. If this is the case, an evacuation may mean no more than walking up a riverbank. However, you should make evacuations part of your pretrip planning. A good start is to leave word—with friends, a nearby ranger station, or on your car—as to what your plans are and when you plan to be off the river. Then consider the following:

• Is there a road alongside the river? If so, is there

enough traffic to hitchhike? How far (and where) will the shuttle vehicles be?

• If there isn't a road, where are the access points? How can you get in and out of them? Is it a road or a trail? How long will it take?

• How can you contact local emergency services, like the sheriff's department or the rescue squad? Include their phone numbers in the first-aid kit. Where is the nearest phone? Do you know enough about the area to tell them where to come?

• Are there other organizations on the river, such as an Outward Bound group or a rafting outfitter, that might be able to help?

If possible, send people in pairs for mutual support. If you have to walk an injured person out, don't send him out by himself. Depending on the seriousness of the injury, send at least one and preferably two people with him. That way, if his condition worsens, one can stay with him while the other person goes for help. If the injury is major and you lack the means to evacuate, you will have to wait to be rescued.

Safety is an integral part of paddling. Almost everything you do in paddling—the way you dress, your paddling technique, even what you think—in some way makes you more or less safe. Your knowledge of water and its hazards will help you stay out of trouble; so will your paddling skills. But at some point, these skills must blend seamlessly into the skills of escape and rescue. If you ignore one aspect or another, it won't be there when you need it. So practice both equally.

ELEVEN

Getting There —and Back

RIVERS, IT SEEMS, are never conveniently located, and with all the preparation for and paraphernalia of boating, just getting going takes a while. If you paddle a lot, you'll spend a lot of time driving. Artist William Nealy has only half-humorously suggested boat stickers that read, "I'd rather be driving."

And you will drive a lot, which brings us to the subject of this chapter. We started this book with water, and I suppose that it's appropriate to end it with the mundane task of getting the canoe *to* water, where it needs to be for you to paddle it. Not only that, we want a vehicle at the end to pick your boat up. We call this activity shuttling, which is a task simple in concept but sometimes difficult in the execution.

Mundane, did I say? Sometimes shuttles are epic, and it has been truly said that the shuttle is the most difficult and dangerous part of a trip. Now, it's no problem if you simply want to run a stretch of river alongside which is a road. Highway builders often obligingly follow river gorges, thereby letting nature do most of the work.

Sometimes it's more difficult. For running the Colorado River through the Grand Canyon, driving from the takeout to the put-in (Diamond Creek to Lee's

TIPS ON SHUTTLES

• Break-ins and rip-offs occur more often in some places than in others. Use a shuttle service if this is a problem. Otherwise, try not to leave anything valuable in the car. Hide your wallet, or a spare credit card, separately.

• Don't take your keys on the river; if you lose them, you're sunk. Keep a spare. A magnetic spare key holder works well.

• If you can't find where the keys are hidden, try rocking the car. Often they will rattle and reveal themselves.

• Leave some water, snacks, and dry clothes in the take-out shuttle car.

• If possible, set the shuttle so that you can pick up all the boats when you finish. You are much fresher when starting out, so that's the time to do all the driving.

• Make a shuttle map. Too often shuttle drivers are sent off without a firm idea of where they are going. "You can't miss it," they said. Oh yeah?

(Illustration by William Nealy, courtesy of Menasha Ridge Press.)

Ferry) takes a full day, and paddlers often choose to fly. Flying is sometimes the only way to get to really remote rivers in places like Alaska. My own candidate for the ultimate shuttle was one I did for a commercial rafting trip in Central America. The put-in was in central Guatemala. Local drivers had proved unreliable, so we drove our own bus from North Carolina down through Mexico and Belize to get there, then dropped off the rafters and drove back north to pick them up in Mexico. The one-way return trip required five days of hard driving on Central American roads, and included crossing two international boundaries (with appropriate hassles from customs officials) each way. We once drove the entire return leg with no brakes!

Finding Your Way

After running a shuttle you can see that finding your way isn't something you do only on the river. Sometimes getting into and out of the takeout can be much more of a challenge. Often the river is Class III and the shuttle Class V. Fortunately, with river running more popular than ever, finding your way is easier than it ever was. There are guidebooks about almost every river in the country, available in every possible format, some even waterproof. They can save you a lot of time and trouble.

Let's go through the whole process of checking out a river from the big picture on down. There isn't much need to go through this whole process in the United States anymore, but you'll still use it in another country.

Start with a good atlas to give yourself an idea of the lay of the land. Then look at the road network to see what it will take to get there. After that, look for a regional guidebook on the river in question. If it's in your own area, you will probably find guidebooks in a club library or in a local outfitter's shop. Be selective: guidebooks vary widely in quality, and some are rather dated.

• How current is the book's information? Rivers sometimes change, along with little things like shuttle roads and highway numbers.

• How difficult is the section you're considering running? Older guidebooks often overrate rapids by today's standards, and sections that were considered unrunnable when the book was written might be considered routine now. On the other hand, much of what passes for a ratings system for rapids is subjective, and varies widely from one part of the country to another. Consider also whether the guidebook was written for open canoes or for decked boats like kayaks.

• How accessible is the river? If it runs through a remote canyon or a wilderness area, how will you get in or out if there is an emergency?

• Can you check the water level? Is there a gauge or a phone number you can call? Many rivers change radically in difficulty as the water level fluctuates, so consider an alternate plan—a different section of river or a different river entirely—if the river you want is too high or low to run.

• How long will the shuttle take? Consider alternatives, like hiring locals to do it. These people are often listed in guidebooks.

If you need more detailed information, then obtain a United States Geological Survey quadrangle. USGS quads are available for the entire country and have a scale (1:24,000) that is suitable for most purposes. But a USGS quad, though useful in finding such unchanging features as contours, ridges, and the like, is probably out of date when it comes to transient features like bridges, houses, trails, and roads. Most of these maps are compiled from aerial surveys and then "field-checked," meaning that someone actually looked at the ground. The Rainey Mountain quadrangle, for example, which covers a good part of the Chattooga River, was field-checked in 1957.

Another source of information—and sometimes problems—is the local populace. Here I mean anyone from the farmer who lives up the road to the paddlers who frequent the area. The paddlers will have more current info about the river, but residents can often save you time in finding shuttle roads. If the river is popular, there is often a paddlers' hangout nearby, or perhaps a rafting outfitter, canoe rental, or outdoor shop.

Don't overlook federal and state agencies (the Bureau of Land Management, the Forest Service) in your search for information. Many of these agencies publish their own maps of the river and the surrounding territory.

Just a few words of caution: don't blindly accept someone else's ideas about what is runnable and what's not. Most people will give you an honest appraisal, but some either won't or can't. The same goes for guidebooks. Guidebook authors and cartographers are quick to point out that their books are intended as general references, *not* as a substitute for scouting. Nothing should substitute for your own judgment.

River Rights

Rivers, flat or white, are a finite resource. Every year rivers are lost to the voracious demands of developers, dam builders, and the like. The rivers left have become a lot more crowded. This has led to problems not only on the river, but off the river as well, in the form of access problems and squabbles. What to do?

First, fight like hell for the rivers that are left. Free rivers, like the once-great herds of buffalo, are on the wane. You are much more effective working in your own community than on high-profile national issues. The best way to make a difference nationally is to join and support river-conservation organizations like American Rivers (see Resources). And write to your congressman and local politicians. Often.

Second, join a national paddling organization like the American Canoe Association. All of us benefit from the ACA's work in river conservation, safety, and the general development of the sport. If you get anything out of paddling, put something back in. White-water enthusiasts should also support the American Whitewater Affiliation. The AWA has recently meta-morphosed into one of the nation's premier river-conservation organizations and does worthwhile work in other areas, like safety, as well.

Third, preserve what rights you already have on the river by acting responsibly. Irresponsible, reckless, and shortsighted behavior closes rivers just as surely as do dams. Act with some consideration for the envi-ronment, your fellow paddlers, and other people on the river.

Access

River access is a complex legal issue. In most cases, few people will dispute your right to be *on* the river. What causes problems is getting on and off it. In most cases you are trespassing if you get out of your boat on private land, even to portage a low-head dam. If you want to set a shuttle or camp overnight, you should certainly check with the landowner. Some are touchier than others, especially if they have had prob-lems like trash, rowdiness, or cut fences in the past. Now we know that *we* would never throw trash on someone's land, but if you don't ask and are the last ones to leave, you will be blamed for whatever is found there. You might even offer to help clean up the area in return for access rights. At the very least, you must always ask permission.

ENVIRONMENTAL AWARENESS. Just as paddling is more than technique, a river is more than a gymnasium—a river is a resource and, for many of us, a way of life. We must preserve it, both in the small picture (the things we do and don't do) and in the big picture of rivers on the national scene.

The small picture is you. Environmental awareness while on the river doesn't begin and end with not lit-tering, or even with picking up other people's trash. Take a look at your boat and equipment. Is everything tied in securely? Any lost piece of gear, especially a stray piece of foam, is just another piece of river trash. It's often surprising to see what boaters leave on the river: old fiberglass patches, pieces of foam from a last-minute trim, and sometimes pieces of thwarts and gunnels. Take it with you!

Some other good ideas:

• Don't take glass or breakable containers on the river.

• Take a trash bag with you on the river; it's easy in a canoe.

• Reduce noise pollution on the river.

• Join a volunteer river clean-up trip.

Finally, environmental awareness is sharing the river with others, which brings us to the next subject: river etiquette.

RIVER ETIQUETTE. The day of the lone voyageur passing through the wilderness is, for the most part, over. It is not unusual for some popular rivers to have three thousand to four thousand people a day traverse a four- to eight-mile stretch. This can be either over-whelming or manageable depending on how you approach it. As with any other group situation, simple courtesy can make the situation tolerable.

Often we forget, in our enthusiasm, that not all river users are paddlers. There are the Elder Race (fisher-men), tubers, and rafters, both private and commercial. All these people have as much right to be there—and enjoy themselves—as you do.

• Fishermen are best left alone; don't paddle up and try to be friendly by asking if they've caught anything: it gets old after the three hundredth time.

• Don't cut into a commercial raft trip. Stay out of their way and let them pass. They generally have a schedule to meet.

• Don't hog the takeout and put-in ramps. Get your boats loaded or unloaded and then move off to the side. Other users will appreciate it.

I am indebted to Dan Langston—the Mister Manners, C. Northcote Parkinson, and Sir Isaac Newton of the river—for the formulation of the following basic laws of river etiquette, which he has kindly consented for me to adopt for this book.

FIRST LAW: *Two river craft cannot occupy the same place on any river at the same time.*

Obvious? Surely. But many paddlers seem bent on disproving it, at least to judge by their actions on the river. One reason seems to be inattention, or attention in the wrong place. Some paddlers concentrate so hard on what's immediately in front of them that they do not look upstream. Remember the Fifth Funda-mental? Expand your vision.

The First Law has a corollary: *Go with the flow or yield to those who do.*

You are responsible for knowing where you are, relative to everyone else, at all times. This is really a communication skill, both between you and the river and between you and others on the river. If you commit yourself to a narrow chute at the same time as another craft, you will collide. If the other craft is a large raft, you will lose. Look upstream before you peel out: the boats upstream of you (who are in the flow) have the right-of-way.

Look downstream, too. Consider Woodall's Theorem of Flow Reversal, which postulates that a watercraft in a hole tends to stay there unless set in motion by 1) a collision with another watercraft or 2) a conscientious effort on the part of the paddler. It's considered bad form, just as it is in ocean surfing, to "drop in" on someone. If you're the one surfing, don't be a hole hog and not let anyone else play. The same goes for camping out at a congested play spot.

Plan where you're going in a rapid, then make sure nobody else is there, especially true if you're an I-can't-stop-now novice. Keep an open eddy (one you can catch) between you and the next boat.

SECOND LAW: *A watercraft in motion tends to remain in motion.*

This is true if there are no eddies to catch or big holes to stop the boat.

The corollary is: *The least maneuverable craft has the downstream right-of-way.* Kayaks are more maneuverable than canoes, canoes than rafts, and so on. You don't want to argue with a raft, anyway. But what about two boats of the same type? Since "least maneuverable" often equals "least skilled," under Langston's Corollary of Compromise, the better boater yields—because he can.

Be aware that skill level makes a difference here. An experienced raft guide may well have much better control than a novice canoeist. Still, in a narrow chute, he probably won't be able to miss you, however hard he might try.

THIRD LAW: *The ability of a river to absorb different-sized groups is directly proportional to the size (and length) of the river.*

The bigger the group, the more water you need to

flush 'em down the river (the basic research for this law was allegedly done by the bathroom fixture industry). Opinions vary widely across the country as to what *crowded* means, and this law must be modified according to geographical customs and notions. Many rivers in the western United States, for example, have strict limits on group sizes and numbers, whereas the rule in the East seems to be the more, the merrier. For most rivers, though, a group of three boats is the minimum recommended for safety reasons, and groups of more than twelve are cumbersome. Larger groups should consider subdividing.

FOURTH LAW: *Foreign behavior is often poorly tolerated by locals.*

You may not truly appreciate the implications of this law (also known as Rambo's Law) until someone fires a shot across your bow or trashes your car. Many of the better river runs are located in rural America, which espouses traditional values not in vogue elsewhere. Public drinking, loud music, nudity, and disregard for local traffic are common complaints about paddlers. Ugly paddlers hurt everybody.

The corollary to this law (as well as the solution to the above problems) is the Golden Rule.

Lifting and Carrying Canoes

Once you're finished, you'll need to get your boat out of the water and onto the car. The big difficulty is the weight of the canoe. Canoes may be wonderfully stable freighters on the river, but they are a pain to carry, even for a short way. Nevertheless, portaging, or carrying, a canoe is one of those cherished romantic traditions associated with the sport (although the romance fades quickly after the first hundred yards or so). It helps, one supposes, to have some French Canadian or Native American blood.

First, there is the problem of getting the boat onto your shoulders. Unless you are fortunate enough to own one of those composite Kevlar wonders, your boat will weigh a minimum of seventy-five to eighty pounds. If it has air bags, a saddle, and the like, it can easily top the hundred-pound mark—a formidable burden if you weigh only a few pounds more.

To lift a canoe, start on the side. Here's where that fitness program really comes in, because you'll need a

Dave Moccia shows the easy way to empty a canoe. With the canoe at the water's edge, push down with one foot on the gunnel nearest shore. At the same time, hook the T-grip of the paddle underneath the gunnel and pull.

Roll the boat up on shore, emptying the water. Grab the gunnel (it's okay to do it here) . . .

and flip the boat all the way over.

certain amount of muscle. You can make the task easier by removing all those things that you tied in earlier.

Move to the center of the canoe, about where the
balance point will be, and grab one of the thwarts. Lift
the canoe, still open side up, to the top of your thighs
at about crotch level. Lean back slightly to transform
your thighs into a platform, and slide one hand next to
your body and the other across the canoe. Now comes
the fun part. Lift one knee to give the boat a push, then
rotate your body *under* the canoe while swinging it
over your head. You should end up with the canoe
above your head and a hand on each side of the
thwart.

This method works equally well (or poorly, depending on how you do) with two people, who hoist opposite ends of the boat.

Another method of lifting the canoe is to pivot the
boat on its bow (or stern) instead of lifting the whole
thing. The movement is virtually the same as described above, but the paddler moves a bit farther forward so that the stern stays on the ground. This reduces the weight that he has to lift and makes the
canoe initially easier to balance. After getting the bow
of the boat over his head, he walks back under the boat

Lifting the solo canoe. First pick the boat straight up so that it rests on the top of your thighs.

Then roll the boat up over your head, turning as you do.

*A somewhat easier method
is to pick up the stern.*

until he reaches the balance point, then tilts the boat forward over him.

Which brings us to the second problem: balance. Some part of the canoe, usually a thwart, has to fit on your shoulders. Sometimes you can hold on to a seat for stability; other times you'll have to grab the gunnels. You may find, especially with a solo canoe, that there is no thwart near the balance point. Try this: tie a pair of paddles lengthwise across two thwarts, with enough space between them to put your head into. The shafts of the paddles rest on your shoulders, allowing you to adjust the balance point. Paddlers who portage a lot often use a *portage yoke*, a specially

Then walk backwards under the boat . . . and tilt it down over you.

shaped thwart that fits over your shoulders. This works great—*if* you can install it in the right place.

Once you have that eighteen-foot canoe over your head, keep in mind that half of it is sticking out on either end. Swing it around and you'll take out everything in a nine-foot radius.

Putting the canoe down is the reverse of picking it up. Two people need to agree on which side to put it down. Say something like, "Off right." If you're walking in front, watch where the bow painter hangs; stepping on it is like tripping on your shoelace.

If you have more people, there are other (and easier) ways of carrying a canoe. Two people can just pick up

A two-person carry is a quick and simple way of moving a boat over short distances. Add a person on either side for a four-person carry.

the canoe by the bow and stern plates and walk off with it. Some manufacturers even include handles for doing this. Four people make it even easier. Two people, one on each side, grab a thwart at the bow, and two take a thwart near the stern. Away they go. The ultimate in decadence, however, is the portage cart, a cradle for the canoe with bicycle wheels on the side. As long as your path is relatively smooth, these contrivances work well, although their use will elicit sneers from the old-timers.

Cartopping

Although it isn't particularly aerodynamic, a canoe will fly quite nicely if it comes off the top of a car at highway speeds, and the idea of its going through someone's windshield doesn't bear thinking about. A crash landing won't do the canoe any good, either. So we want it to stay on the car. How exactly do we manage that?

By far the easiest way is with cartop racks designed for the purpose. If you're flush, you can buy some excellent all-purpose rack systems, like the Yakima. These will, with the proper attachments, also carry your skis, bicycle, and luggage. Or you can make your own with hooks (manufactured by Quick & Easy) that clamp on to the rain gutters and bolt to a two-by-four crosspiece.

However, any contraption that keeps the canoe off the top of the car (and thus off the paint) and can be tied securely will work. I have successfully used contoured foam blocks that slide over the gunnels to cushion the canoe on the roof, with some stamped metal hooks that clip under the rain gutters to anchor the lines going over the boat. We once tied eight boats (six kayaks and two very large C-1s) on a full-size Detroit sedan without any racks at all. An old blanket padded the roof, and we tied the boats by running the rope through the windows. To be sure, this also tied the doors shut so that we had to enter and leave the car via the windows, but what the hey, it was a paddlin' road trip!

Some other tips:

• If you get boat racks, beware of making the crosspieces too long—a temptation if you carry wide canoes. Getting out of the car, you may bonk yourself in the head.

• Tie the boats down in four places: twice over the hull (one rope at each rack) and at the bow and stern. In the unlikely event that both hull ties come loose, or even if the racks come off, the bow and stern ties would still keep the boat from flying away.

• Use a tension knot so that you can really crank

(Illustration by William Nealy, courtesy of Menasha Ridge Press.)

things down tight. A trucker's hitch works well because you can readily untie it later. If you have to get in and out of the hood or back of your car or truck frequently, try a tautline hitch for the bow and stern tie.

And finally, be patient. Nothing ruins a trip faster than trouble on the shuttle, be it an accident, a hassle with a local farmer, or just getting lost.

Resources

American National Red Cross. *Canoeing*. New York. Doubleday & Co., 1977, 1981.

This book's primary orientation is toward recreational lake canoeing.

Anderson, Bob. *Stretching*. Bolinas, CA. Shelter Publications, 1980.

The standard reference on the subject. Every paddler should own a copy *and use it*.

Bechdel, Les, and Slim Ray. *River Rescue*. Boston. Appalachian Mountain Club, 1985, 1989.

The standard reference on the subject, as well as on river safety. Every paddler should have a copy. The second edition is a completely revised book.

Davidson, James West, and John Rugge. *The Complete Wilderness Paddler*. New York. Alfred A. Knopf, 1977.

The definitive work on wilderness tripping. An unexpected bonus is the excellent writing. Some of the more technical aspects of the book are outdated, but it still comes highly recommended.

Foshee, John. *Solo Canoeing*. Harrisburg, PA. Stackpole Books, 1988.

Foster, Thomas. *Recreational Whitewater Canoeing*.

Books

Miller's Falls, MA. Leisure Enterprises, 1978, 1981.
Tom Foster is the ACA's instruction chairman and runs the Outdoor Center of New England.

Gullion, Laurie. *Canoeing and Kayaking Instruction Manual.* Newington, VA. American Canoe Association, 1987.
The official ACA instruction manual. The information is excellent, but kayaks are stuffed in with canoes.

Harrison, Dave. *Sports Illustrated Canoeing.* New York. Harper and Row, 1981, 1988.

Jacobson, Cliff. *The New Wilderness Canoeing and Camping.* Merrillville, IN. ICS Books, 1986.
Though I take issue with some of Cliff's paddling techniques, the sections on camping and portaging are excellent. Worth reading if you're really into tripping.

McNair, Robert, L. Matty, and Paul Landry. *Basic River Canoeing.* Martinsville, IN. American Camping Association, 1968, 1985.
A classic work, still worth reading, but showing its age.

Mason, Bill. *Path of the Paddle.* Minocqua, WI. North Word Press, 1980.
Song of the Paddle. Minocqua, WI. North Wood Press, 1988.
The late Bill Mason's position in the world of canoeing is similar to that of St. Peter in the Catholic Church. If you're into classic canoeing, read his books. Modern whitewater techniques differ somewhat, however, from those used by Bill in his esteemed Chestnut.

Nealy, William. *Kayak.* Birmingham, AL. Menasha Ridge Press, 1986.
Nealy's madcap drawings are always amusing, but this book conveys serious information in a very readable way. The sections on hydrology and rescue are worth anyone's time.

Penny, Richard. *The Whitewater Sourcebook.* Birmingham, AL. Menasha Ridge Press, 1989.
The bible of white water, Penny's book covers nearly every whitewater stream in the United States. Much good information in here about stream flows, difficulty, and managing agencies.

Twain, Mark. *Life on the Mississippi*. New York. New
   American Library, 1961.

Videos

The Pivot Point.
   Produced by the NOC instructional staff, this film
   provides a visual reinforcement for the strokes in
   this book. Highly recommended as a companion
   piece.
The C-1 Challenge.
   If you're looking at C-1s, look at this film first. Pro-
   duced by former World Team champion Kent Ford, it
   gives an excellent look at what it's like to paddle a
   decked boat.
Citizen Racer's Workshop.
   Nantahala Outdoor Center
   US 19W, Box 41
   Bryson City, NC 28713
   Also by Kent Ford, this video presents the basics of
   citizen's racing. Although mostly oriented toward
   decked boats, some of the techniques are adaptable
   to open boats as well.
Margin for Error.
The Uncalculated Risk.
Whitewater Primer.
   American Red Cross
   17th and D Sts.
   Washington, DC 20006
   Three river safety films every paddler should see.
   Most club libraries have these.
Cold, Wet, and Alive.
   American Canoe Association
   P.O. Box 1190
   Newington, VA 22122-1190
   New ACA film on hypothermia. Another must-see.
River Rescue: the Video.
   Gravity Sports Films
   100 Broadway
   Jersey City, NJ 07306
   Despite being somewhat arcane, this film is worth
   seeing as you move into white water. It provides an
   overview of the field.
The Drowning Machine.
   Film Space
   615 Clay St.

State College, PA 16801

The classic film about low-head dams.

Waterwalker.

Song of the Paddle.

Path of the Paddle Whitewater.

Path of the Paddle Quiet Water.

North Word Press

Box 1360

Minocqua, WI 54548

Excellent, lyrical camera work of the North Woods distinguishes all of Mason's films—worth watching for this reason alone. *Song of the Paddle* and *Path of the Paddle* are film versions of his books; *Waterwalker* (Mason's last film) stands alone. As with Mason's books, these are oriented toward canoe tripping, and you will find some substantial differences between Mason's treatment of strokes and white water and the techniques presented in this book.

L. L. Bean Guide to Canoeing.

L. L. Bean

Freeport, ME 04033

An excellent beginning guide with veteran instructor and paddler Ken Stone.

Books, Accessories, and Equipment

ACA Book Service, Box 1190, Newington, VA 22122

ACA Film Library, Box 1190, Newington, VA 22122

Carries most of the videos and books listed here.

Nantahala Outdoor Center Outfitter's Store, US 19W, Box 41, Bryson City, NC 28713; 800 367-3521

Purveyors of high-quality gear, including books and NOC videos. The salesmen can also give you a straight answer about canoes and accessories. Free catalog.

Four Corners Marine, P.O. Box 379, Durango, CO 81302; 303 259-3893

An excellent mail-order house. Though the staffers cater primarily to whitewater paddlers, they also speak open canoe.

The Canoe Shopper *(Canoe Magazine)*, P.O. Box 3418, Kirkland, WA 98083; 800 MY-CANOE

The retail arm of *Canoe Magazine* carries a curious blend of useless gewgaws and good stuff. Reasonable selection of books and videos.

L. L. Bean, Freeport, ME 04033
L. L. Bean needs no introduction. They carry a wide selection of canoeing gear, books, and videos (including their own).

Menasha Ridge Press, P.O. Box 59257, Birmingham, AL 35359-9257
America's premier river guidebook publisher, Menasha covers rivers flat and white nationwide. A good place to start looking if you're researching a river.

Appalachian Mountain Club, 5 Joy St., Boston, MA 02108
AMC has a long tradition of guidebooks going back to the thirties. Most of the listings are for the Northeast.

Canoe Instruction

Nantahala Outdoor Center, US 19W, Box 41, Bryson City, NC 28713, 704 488-2175
The college of whitewater knowledge. NOC has no equal for whitewater canoe and kayak instruction. As a teaching institution, it has been compared to Oxford and Julliard.

Outdoor Center of New England, 8 Pleasant St., Miller's Falls, MA 01349; 413 659-3926
Founder Tom Foster is the chairman of the ACA's National Instruction Committee.

Clubs

A directory of state and local clubs can be found in the *ACA Canoeing and Kayaking Instruction Manual.*

Organizations

American Canoe Association, P.O. Box 1190, Newington, VA 22122-1190
America's largest and most active canoesport organization.

American Rivers, 801 Pennsylvania Ave. S.E., Suite 303, Washington, DC 20003

American Whitewater Affiliation, 146 N. Brockway, Palatine, IL 60067
As the name suggests, the AWA is oriented toward whitewater paddling. It has lately become a strong force for river conservation.

U.S. Canoe Association, 4169 Middlebrook Dr., Dayton, OH 45440-3311

The core of the USCA is marathon racing in the Midwest, but it also supports recreational paddling and river conservation.

Appalachian Mountain Club, 5 Joy St., Boston, MA 02108

America's oldest conservation and outdoor recreation organization (founded in 1876), the AMC sponsors a strong paddling club system. Well worth investigating if you live in the East.

Magazines

Canoe Magazine, P.O. Box 3418, Kirkland, WA 98083

America's most successful canoeing magazine, *Canoe* attempts—sometimes successfully—to cover it all. A subscription is a worthwhile investment for any paddler.

Paddler, P.O. Box 635, Oscoda, MI 48750

With veteran editor Harry Roberts at the helm, *Paddler* incorporates former *River Runner* and *Canoesport Journal* to cover both whitewater and flatwater canoeing. A free companion tabloid, *Paddling*, can be found at many outfitting stores.

American Whitewater, 146 N. Brockway, Palatine, IL 60067

Membership magazine of the AWA. Good conservation and safety articles mixed with difficult paddling and squirt boating.

The American Canoeist, P.O. Box 1190, Newington, VA 22122

Informational membership magazine of the ACA.

Index

Page numbers in italics refer to illustrations.